Traveling to Bahamas

A Local Guide to New Providence and Nassau Paradise Islands

Author
SAMPSON UZO JERRY

Contributors
Louisa Jerry
Onyekachi Marvellous Jerry

Publisher
GLOBAL PRINT DIGITAL
Arlington Row Bibury Cirencester, GL7 5NJ
United Kingdom

ISBN: 978-1-3999-1866-4

Copyright Notice

The entire content of this book is copyrighted including the cover image, and any illegal use of this book is prohibited, such as copying either physical or digital, printing, unauthorized distribution and sales. Its distribution is limited to the authorized distributors and retailers who are in relationship with the author or legal marketers. Violation of this right is punishable under international copyright law.

Allright Reserve Global Print Digital Publication, Copyright © 2022

DEDICATION

My beloved Wife is behind the motivation that brought this book to a success, she took whole responsibility of our daily job while I had to travel from place to place to get the accurate information that made up this Travel book. I dedicate this successful work to Her. I thank my Eight Months old Son who knew he had to sleep at the right time while I do the needful.

CONTENT

DEDICATION .... A
THE BAHAMAS 1

Introduction 1
   Geography 3
   The Landforms and Relief 4
      The Bahamas' weather 6
      Animal and plant life are both abundant. 7

The People of Bahamas 8
   Groups and ethnicity,The languages, and Spritual faith 8
   Form of Settlement 9

The Bahamas Economy 10
   Farming and fishing 11
   Manufacturing, Resources and power 12
   Trade, Services and finance 12
   Transportation 14

Bahamas Political Governance and society 15
   Constitutional framework 15
   The Political process and Education 16
   Wellbeing and health 18

Bahamas Cultural, lifestyle and Social Customs 20
   The arts and cultural Establishments 22
   Recreational activities and sports 24

The History of Bahama Islands 25
   British Foundation 27
   The Political Freedom of the The Bahamas 34

New Providence Islands 40

- Nassau Paradise Island 43
  - The Orientation 43
  - Nassau History Overview 45
  - Best Traveling Period and the Climate Information 50
  - Hotels and Lodging 52
  - Transportation and Car Rental 55
  - Nassau International Airport 59
  - Tourism 63
    - Things you can Do in Nassau Bahamas 69
    - Interesting Things to Do in Nassau 83
    - Top Things to See in Nassau Bahamas 92
    - Social Tour of Nassau 100
    - Favourite Attractions 103
      - Tourist Attractions 103
      - Beaches 113
      - Landmarks and Monuments 115
      - Museums 119
      - Art Galleries 124
      - Attractions Nearby 126
    - Things to Do 131
      - Medical Tourism 131
      - Events and Festivals 135
      - Restaurants and Dining 141
      - Shopping 144
- Paradise Island 146
  - New Providence and Paradise Islands Restaurants 149

The Bahamas
Introduction

The Bahamas is an archipelago and country off the coast of the Western Hemisphere. In 1973, The Bahamas, which had previously been a British territory, became a Commonwealth country. Although some historians believe it is derived from the Spanish bajamar, which means "shallow water," the name Bahamas is of Lucayan Taino (Arawakan) origin. The islands command a strategic position as the entry point to the Gulf of Mexico, the Caribbean Sea, and the Central American region. The Bahamas' strategic location has given the country's history a distinct and frequently spectacular character. It was there that Christopher Columbus first set foot in the New World.. While the early attempts at European-dominated settlement were marked by intense national rivalries, interspersed with extended periods of anarchy and piracy, the fate of the peaceful indigenous inhabitants remains one of the more tragic incidents in the region's development.

As a result, The Bahamas' society and culture are a unique blend of European and African heritages, with the latter being a legacy of the slave trade and the advent of the plantation system using African slaves. The islands, which have few natural resources other than a pleasant climate and beautiful beaches, have become increasingly reliant on the money generated by the extensive tourist amenities and financial industry that have developed, frequently as a result of foreign capital input. The islands' continuous appeal with tourists, primarily from North America, has helped to keep the people, the majority of whom are of African heritage, at a reasonably high quality of life.. Nassau, the capital, situated on New Providence Island, which is tiny yet significant.

Geography

The archipelago, which lies to the north of Cuba and Hispaniola, is made up of roughly 700 islands and cays, only about 30 of which are inhabited, as well as over 2,000 low, barren rock formations. It stretches more than 500 miles (800 kilometers) southeast-northwest between Grand Bahama Island, which covers 530 square miles (1,373 square kilometers) and is located about 60 miles (100 kilometers) off the southeastern coast of Florida, and Great Inagua Island, which is located about 50 miles (80 kilometers) from Cuba's eastern tip. The Out (Family) Islands are the islands that are not part of New Providence. Grand Bahama, which includes the important communities of Freeport and West End; and Andros, the biggest island at 2,300 square miles [6,000 square kilometers]. Eleuthera (187 square miles [484 square km]), the location of one of the first efforts at colonization in the Bahamas; Abaco, or Great Abaco (372 square miles [963 square km]); and Abaco, or Great Abaco (372 square miles [963 square]).

The Landforms and Relief

The Bahamas are located on an uneven undersea tableland that rises from the Atlantic Ocean's depths and is isolated from surrounding territories to the south and west by deepwater waterways. The main islands' prominent topographic characteristics include extensive regions of flatland, often only a few feet in height; the Bimini group, for example, has a maximum elevation of about 20 feet (6 metres). On the northeastern side of a number of islands facing the Atlantic, a range or series of ranges of hills line the islands' longer axis. Sand washed ashore and pushed inland by trade winds creates these mountains. Sand dunes are usually seen near the coast on the younger hills. The solidity rises as you get closer to the center, when the particles cement together to create Bahama limestone. The islands of Eleuthera and Long Island (230 square miles [596 square kilometers]) contain the most hills above 100 feet (30 metres). Mount Alvernia, the Bahamas' highest point at 206 feet (63 meters), is located on Cat Island (150 square miles [388 square km]). The islands are made up of limestone rock and the skeletal remnants of coral fossils and other marine species beneath the soil. There are no rivers, although there are enormous lakes on numerous islands, including New Providence, San Salvador (63 square miles [163 square km]), and Great Inagua. Andros Island has plenty of fresh water.

The Bahamas' weather

One of the area's major draws is the moderate Bahamian temperature throughout the year. The average temperature ranges from the low 70s Fahrenheit (about 21 degrees Celsius) in the winter to the low 80s Fahrenheit (about 27 degrees Celsius) in the summer, with extremes rarely falling below the low 60s Fahrenheit (about 16 degrees Celsius) or rising above the low 90s Fahrenheit (about 32 degrees Celsius). The average annual rainfall is roughly 44 inches (1,120 mm), with the most of it falling during the summer. Prevailing winds, which come from the northeast in the winter and the southeast in the summer, help to cool a humid atmosphere. Tropical cyclones (hurricanes) are a hazard from

June to November, and they have caused significant damage on occasion.

Animal and plant life are both abundant.

On the islands of Grand Bahama, Abaco, Andros, and New Providence, there are extensive and gorgeous Caribbean pine woods. On several of the islands, there are also hardwood forests. Shrubs and low trees dominate the woody vegetation elsewhere. Frogs, lizards, and snakes, all of which are nonpoisonous, predominate in animal life, while caves along the more rocky beaches are home to numerous kinds of bats. The agouti, a rodent, the raccoon, the iguana, and the beautiful flamingo, the national bird, are among the larger creatures. All of them have had their numbers and distribution drastically decreased. Several animals from Europe, including sheep, horses, and other livestock, have also been introduced. Fish and other edible marine species, such as conch and lobster, thrive in the nearby seas.

The People of Bahamas
Groups and ethnicity, The languages, and Spritual faith

The Bahamians are proud of their background and do not hesitate to display it. They will engage in engaging discourse about practically anything bahamian if given the chance. From regattas, fishing, and flag colors to culture, religion, and food. Bahamians are warm-hearted and soulful, as well as helpful and informed. The Bahamas' population is predominantly of African heritage. A small but considerable minority of people of mixed European and African ancestry, as well as descendants of English pioneer settlers and loyalist refugees from the American Revolution, live in the area. Although English is the only native language of Bahamians, French or the related Haitian Creole vernacular is spoken due to the influx of Haitian immigrants since the mid-twentieth century. A large number of Bahamians belong to Christian churches; the majority are non-Anglican Protestants, with Roman Catholics and Anglicans making up lesser shares.

Form of Settlement

On each island, population centers are dispersed extensively. Cat Island, for example, is positioned leeward, where it is tranquil and protected. Others, like the Abaco Cays, face the north and northeast, where they are exposed to the northeast trade winds (the cays off Abaco and Little Abaco islands). Main communities are generally found where there is a natural harbor or at least maritime access. The population has shifted dramatically from fishing and rural communities to tourism and economic hotspots. The islands of New Providence, Grand Bahama, and Abaco have seen the most population shift (Great Abaco).

Approximately two-thirds of Bahamians live on New Providence Island, which, along with Grand Bahama and Abaco, has seen the biggest internal migration. Because of immigration from the United States and other West Indian islands, the country's population growth rate is substantially greater than the Caribbean average. The Caribbean region's natural population growth rate is roughly average, while birth and mortality rates are lower than the average for the West Indies as a whole..

The Bahamas Economy

Despite the concentration of the people in tourist-oriented

metropolitan centers (primarily Nassau and Freeport), the traditional pattern of small-scale farming and fishing continues in several communities, particularly in the southeastern islands. The Bahamas' economy is mostly market-based and mainly reliant on tourism and international financial services. The region's gross national product (GNP) per capita is among the highest.

Farming and fishing

Agriculture contributes a modest percentage of GDP and employs a similar fraction of the labor. Only a small percentage of the land is arable, and the soils are thin. Almost all of the country's food is imported, with the majority coming from the United States. Many fruits, such as tomato, papaya, banana, mangoes, guava, sapodilla (the fruit of a tropical evergreen tree), soursop, grapefruit, and sea grape, thrive in the sunny climate. Pigs, sheep, and cattle are among the animals farmed. Spiny lobster, grouper, and conch dominate the small-scale fishing industry's catch.

Manufacturing, Resources and power

The manufacturing of salt and cement are the only mineral industries that exist. Foreign gasoline and liquefied natural gas are used exclusively to create electricity. On the islands, power plants may be found all throughout. Rum and other alcoholic beverages are produced by manufacturing industries. Cement and medicines are among the other products produced, as well as canned fruits and frozen spiny lobster. Manufacturers are exempt from tariffs and other taxes under the Industries Encouragement Act of 1970..

Trade, Services and finance

The United States is by far the country's most significant commercial partner. China, Panama, Ireland, the US Virgin Islands, Turks and Caicos, the United Kingdom, and Japan are among the other commercial partners. Machinery and transport equipment, food, and mineral fuels are all major imports. Petroleum and rock lobster are the two most important exports. Under the Generalized System of Preferences, the European Union and a number of other nations exclude some Bahamian items from duty.

Tourism contributes more than a third of the country's GDP and employs almost two-fifths of the workforce. It is centered on the islands of New Providence and Grand Bahama, with the majority of visitors coming from the United States. Hundreds of banks and trust businesses have been drawn to The Bahamas because there are no income or corporation taxes, and financial activities are kept private. The government's reliance on indirect taxes, particularly on tourism and foreign commerce, limits public spending. The Bahamas' central bank, the Central Bank of The Bahamas, was founded in 1974. The Bahamian dollar is the official currency, however US dollars are accepted across the islands.

Transportation

Nassau and Freeport, as well as the majority of the populated islands, have paved roads. Between Nassau and the Out Islands, a fleet of tiny motor vessels known as mail boats transports passengers, freight, and mail. The country's two main ports are Nassau and Freeport. A big container transshipment port is also located at Freeport. Every year, a large number of international passenger and freight ships dock in Bahamian ports. There are hundreds of airports on the islands, each with its own set of amenities and services. The majority of them solely offer interisland flights, although international airports may be found in Nassau, Freeport, and Exuma, and international flights can also be found on numerous other Bahamian islands.

Bahamas Political Governance and society

Constitutional framework

The Bahamas' constitution, which was approved in 1973 after the country's independence, is based on the Westminster model, which is used in the United Kingdom. The bicameral parliament is made up of two chambers: the House of Assembly and the Senate, which has fewer authority than the House. The British monarch, who is represented by a governor-general, is the nominal head of state. The governor-general formally appoints the prime minister as the head of government. The prime minister must be a member of the House of Assembly and have a majority of the chamber's votes. Members of the House are chosen by universal adult suffrage, while senators are appointed by the governor. The duration of legislature is five years, but if the prime minister is unable to maintain a majority in the House, or if the House is dissolved and early elections are called, new elections may be conducted sooner. The Court of Appeal, the Supreme Court, and magistrates' courts have judicial authority in the islands, with the Judicial Committee of the Privy Council in the United Kingdom serving as the ultimate court of appeal..

The Political process and Education

All Bahamians aged 18 and above are eligible to vote. Until the early 1950s, Bahamians, particularly women, were mostly unpoliticized. The franchise was not granted to women until 1962. Following the 1960s, improved educational possibilities brought about significant changes. In 1982, the first woman was elected to the House of Commons. There have been female cabinet ministers, parliamentarians, and Supreme Court judges since that period. The Progressive Liberal Party (PLP; founded 1953), which led the majority government movement in the 1950s and 1960s, and the Free National Movement (FNM; formed 1972), which came out of the PLP, are the two main political parties..

Schooling is obligatory from the age of five to sixteen and is free in government schools. The majority of schools are operated by the government, however there are also private and sectarian schools. More than nine out of 10 people are literate. The College of The Bahamas, located in Nassau, was founded in 1974 and provides associate and bachelor's degrees in most fields, as well as master's degrees in a select few topics. It also collaborates with other universities, such as the University of the West Indies, Florida International University, and the University of Miami, to provide programs. A hotel training school supported by the government and the hotel sector, as well as the Bahamas Law School of the University of the West Indies, are among the higher-level schools.

Wellbeing and health

Malnutrition and disabling illnesses are uncommon among Bahamians, and children's medical issues are mostly caused by common infections. Increased alcohol and drug misuse, obesity, and HIV/AIDS have all become major issues, and elderly care has become a major issue. In the second part of the twentieth century, life expectancy improved dramatically and is now equivalent to that of neighboring Caribbean countries.

The Bahamas' Department of Health and Social Development oversees public health services through community clinics and provides home and district nursing as well as disease monitoring. On Grand Bahama and the adjacent cays, there are many public hospitals in Nassau and Freeport, as well as rural health clinics. Nassau and Freeport each have their own private hospitals. The Department of Environmental Health Services is in charge of environmental management, regulation, and conservation.

Although the growth of the tourist and banking industries has improved the daily economic situations of many Bahamians, wealth distribution remains exceedingly unequal. The fact that the poorest and least educated have the largest families and reside in the most congested and economically devastated neighborhoods exacerbates the issue. This pattern frequently results in societal issues, such as an increase in crime and family disturbance. The government has attempted to solve the issue by funding large-scale housing initiatives..

Bahamas Cultural, lifestyle and Social Customs

The culture of the Bahamas includes a mix of African and European influences. People from the Caribbean and the Americas have also affected it. Social conventions and daily life: Most Bahamians value their families, however the number of official weddings declined in the late twentieth century. A single woman, generally the mother, is leading an increasing number of homes. Women were traditionally stay-at-home moms and spouses before the 1940s. Most women now work outside the house as a result of greater educational options and the growth of the tourist sector.

Furthermore, by the late twentieth century, Bahamian women had begun to rise to the top of the public sector, finance, law, medicine, politics, and other fields.

A maid or domestic worker is frequently employed by middle- and upper-class Bahamian homes. Housework is shared by poorer households. Grits, potatoes, bread, conch, fish, spiny lobster, chicken, and foreign meats are all staple meals. Peas and rice, potato salad, macaroni and cheese, cracked conch, conch salad, fried and steamed fish, and fried chicken are among national specialties. A typical dessert is guava duff, a cooked fruit and bread concoction served with a butter sauce. The asue (a collective savings group), friendly societies and lodges, a long tradition of storytelling, and the usage of bush medicine are all examples of folk practices. Junkanoo, the principal festival and celebration, stands out among traditional group activities.

Annual Junkanoo parades, or "rush outs," are staged in Nassau and in several of the Out Islands on Boxing Day and New Year's Day. The main procession takes place on Bay Street in Nassau, with thousands of junkanoos, men dressed in colorful costumes fringed with crepe paper and embellished with beads, feathers, and sequins. To the throbbing beats of goatskin drums, cowbells, whistles, horns, and brass instruments, participants create music and dance. The finest costumes, music, dancing, and theme depiction all receive awards.

The arts and cultural Establishments

Folklore in the Bahamas includes tales of the chickcharney, a three-toed, human-faced creature, the workings of obia (obeah), a folk religion based on witchcraft, and folktales involving the characters B'Booky, B'Rabbit, and B'Anansi (see trickster tale). Religious songs or spirituals, such as waking, or "setting up," songs with biblical themes, are sung during big social events and wakes. Also popular are rhyming songs (both religious and secular). Classic ring dances and quadrilles are still popular, as is dancing to the beat of goombay (also known as rake and scrape), calypso, or soca (a mix of traditional calypso and Indian rhythmic instruments).

The arts, such as painting, sculpture, and photography, as well as crafts, have flourished in The Bahamas, and the country now boasts numerous major organizations dedicated to their development. Dramas, musicals, and dance acts are performed in the Dundas Centre for the Performing Arts in Nassau. A number of galleries, notably the National Art Gallery, which is housed in a mansion overlooking Nassau Harbour, display art and crafts. The Department of Archives is responsible for preserving and making public documents accessible. Antiquities, Monuments, and Museums Corporation is in charge of antiquities, monuments, museums, and archaeology. In Nassau, the Bahamas Historical Society runs a museum and publishes a scholarly magazine..

Recreational activities and sports

The Bahamas are known for their extensive stretches of sand, crystal blue seas, and beautiful coral reefs. Divers visit the islands not just to see the colorful coral gardens, sharks, rays, moray eels, and other plentiful underwater life, but also to examine the countless shipwrecks that are a legacy of the region's treacherous shallow waters and raiding pirates. Snorkeling, windsurfing, deep-sea fishing, and sailing are other popular water activities, and almost every inhabited island has an annual sailing regatta or fishing competition. The islands provide miles of gorgeous deserted beaches and gently reef-protected seas for those who prefer less difficult water activities. Exuma Cays Land and Sea Park is one of the two dozen national parks in the Bahamas that the Bahamas National Trust is concerned with preserving (established 1959). As one might assume given the islands' historical ties to the United Kingdom, many Bahamians play and watch cricket and football (soccer). Basketball is becoming increasingly popular. Athletics (track and field), tennis, and sailing are other sports in which Bahamians have excelled. In 1952, the Bahamas Olympic Association was established..

The History of Bahama Islands

On his first trip to the New World, Christopher Columbus landed somewhere in the Bahamas on October 12, 1492. It is largely assumed that he originally landed on an island known as Guanahani by the natives, which Columbus dubbed San Salvador. The exact location is still a matter of debate; some academics believe it was Samana Cay or Cat Island, while others say it was San Salvador (also known as Watling Island). Columbus, in any event, visited the island and others close before sailing to Cuba and Hispaniola. The Bahamians were a peaceful people who spoke an Arawakan language. They were Lucayan Tainos who had established the archipelago from Hispaniola around 800 CE.

Despite the fact that Columbus gained official control of the islands in the name of Spain, and the islands remained within the Spanish sphere of influence after the Treaty of Tordesillas between Spain and Portugal in 1494, the Spanish made little effort to populate them. Between 1492 and 1508, Spanish raids abducted roughly 40,000 indigenous to labor in

Hispaniola's mines, leaving the islands desolate for more than a century until the first English settlement.

British Foundation

Charles I handed Robert Heath, England's attorney general, possessions in America in 1629, including "Bahama and all other Isles and Islands lying southerly there or neare unto the foresayd continent." Heath, on the other hand, made no attempt to colonize the Bahamas. Nonetheless, in the 1640s, religious tensions amongst English colonists in Bermuda drew the Bahamas into the mix. Capt. William Sayle, a two-time governor of Bermuda, assumed command of an expedition in 1647 to find an island where dissenters might worship as they wanted. The Company of Eleutherian Adventurers was founded in London in July of that year "for the Plantation of the Eleutheria Islands, previously known as Buhama in America, and the Adjacent Islands." Sayle and a group of roughly 70 potential settlers traveled from Bermuda to the Bahamas before October 1648, comprised mostly of Bermudan religious Independents and a few visitors from England. Although the exact location of their arrival is unknown, it is widely assumed that they landed on Eleuthera, which was then known as Cigatoo. They had hoped to develop a thriving plantation colony, but barren land, internal strife, and Spanish meddling put paid to their plans. Sayle and a few other settlers returned to Bermuda.

A fresh group of Bermudans arrived in New Providence around 1666. Charles II gave eight of his cronies as lords proprietors of South Carolina, on the continent of North America, in 1663, and they later nominated Sayle as the state's first governor. Sayle and a few others who were interested in the development of New Providence independently aroused the attention of the lords proprietors to the Bahama Islands' prospects. As a result, in 1670, Charles II granted the duke of Albemarle and five others a gift of the islands, and they took nominal responsibility for the civil administration. The capital was moved to New Providence, which had the biggest population and a protected harbor.

The owners were uninterested in the colonization or development of the islands, which quickly became a sanctuary for pirates, whose assaults on Spanish ships prompted frequent and brutal retaliation raids. The proprietors chose John Wentworth as the first governor in 1671. Despite the fact that detailed instructions for the colony's governance were published and a parliamentary system of government was established, the governor's and settlers' lives were far from simple. New Providence was often conquered by Spaniards, either alone or in tandem with the French, and any governor seeking to impose some sort of law and order was met with hostility by the settlers, who had discovered that piracy was the most lucrative vocation. In 1684, King Charles II intervened and ordered the passage of a legislation against the pirates, although it appears to have had little impact.

Official representations for direct crown rule were made as early as the 17th century. In 1717, the lords proprietors handed over the civil and military governments to the king and leased the islands to Capt. Woodes Rogers, whom the king appointed as the first royal governor and entrusted with exterminating pirates and restoring more stable conditions. About 1,000 pirates surrendered and accepted the king's amnesty when he arrived in 1718, equipped with a disciplined force of troops, while eight unrepentant pirates were executed. The colony was able to adopt the motto "Expulsis piratis restituta commercia" ("Pirates repulsed, commerce restored") as a result of Rogers' actions.

Charles Towne was founded in 1660 and called after Charles II, but when William III ascended to the throne, the name was changed to Nassau; the German area Nassau was a possession of William's family. The settlers wanted an assembly after the restoration of order following the installation of the royal administration. Rogers issued a proclamation convening a representative assembly in 1729, functioning under the authority of the crown, and the colony's administration continued in an orderly fashion from then on, with the exception of occasional pauses caused by enemy invasion.

The town of Nassau was taken by the United States Navy in 1776 while searching for supplies during the American Revolution; they were forced to flee after a few days. The colony succumbed to Spain in May 1782. Although the preliminary provisions of the Peace of Paris returned it to Britain in January 1783, it was skillfully regained in April by loyalist commander Col. Andrew Devaux before news of the peace was received. Many loyalists fled from the United States to the Bahamas when the American Revolution ended, taking advantage of the crown's generous conditions. Lord Dunmore, a former governor of New York and Virginia who served as governor of the Bahamas from 1786 to 1797, was one of the immigrants. Slaves were introduced to the islands by loyalists who escaped to the islands, increasing the population. The cotton plantations they established, which employed slave labor, produced effectively for a few years before succumbing to soil exhaustion, insect pest predation, and, eventually, the abolition of slavery. The lords proprietors sold their remaining rights for £12,000 in 1787.

During the years leading up to abolition, the Bahama Islands, like the rest of the Caribbean, saw a number of slave revolts. The assembly's efforts to frustrate the executive's attempts to improve slave circumstances lasted until August 1, 1834, when the United Kingdom Abolition Act took effect in the province; complete freedom followed in 1838. In 1841, royal letters patent established a legislative council.

Following liberation, the West Indies experienced a period of hardship and disappointment. Former slaves and masters battled for survival. Many went back to subsistence farming, while others stayed on their old owners' property and worked on a share system. There was just a little amount of circulation of. Blockade-running during the American Civil War (1861–65) and the handling of booze during Prohibition in the United States in the 1920s brought significant income to the islands (see prohibition). This activity, on the other hand, produced little long-term contribution to the islands and did not develop a stable economic basis. Many attempts to cultivate pineapples, citrus fruits, tobacco, tomatoes, and sisal for export before and during these times failed, despite initial promise. In 1938, sponge fishing likewise came to an end. Finally, following WWII, intense attempts to establish tourism as the economy's foundation were resoundingly successful, altering the islands' economic and social structures.

The Political Freedom of the The Bahamas

Since the first assembly in 1729, Bahamians have enjoyed great political authority over their affairs. A meeting was organized in London in May 1963 to discuss a new constitution for the islands. The colony was then granted complete internal self-government, with the governor's responsibilities reserved exclusively for foreign affairs, defense, and internal security. On January 7, 1964, the new constitution went into effect, and in 1969, constitutional achievements moved the country closer to total self-government..

The Progressive Liberal Party (PLP) was founded in 1953 by Bahamians of African origin to oppose the ruling party, which replied in 1958 with its own party, the United Bahamian Party (UBP), governed by British-descended MPs. The PLP escalated the clamor for majority rule as the political fight continued. The climax occurred during the 1967 general elections, when the PLP, led by Lynden Pindling, was able to create a government with a slim majority. In general, the PLP supported for tighter government economic control, more Bahamian ownership of businesses, and the replacement of foreign labor with Bahamians. Despite bipartisan support for the path toward self-governance, certain elements argued that ultimate independence should be delayed until after 1973, the year set by the PLP government.

The Commonwealth of the Bahamas was established in 1969, but when the country gained independence on July 10, 1973, the official name was changed to The Commonwealth of The Bahamas. The PLP remained the majority party when the country gained independence. The Free National Movement (FNM), created in 1972 by a merger of the UBP and disgruntled anti-independence PLP members calling themselves the Free PLP, was the major opposition. The administration launched initiatives to boost economic development, raise living standards, and slow the rate of unemployment. The Bahamas is a member of the Caribbean Community and Common Market (Caricom), the United Nations (1973), UNESCO (1981), the Organization of American States (1982), and the Commonwealth (since 1983). (1973).

In the late 1980s, allegations of government complicity with drug traffickers became a serious problem, threatening PLP authority. Another severe and ongoing issue has been the influx of legal and illegal immigrants from Haiti, which has put a strain on the country's social and economic resources. The FNM surged to victory in the August 1992 general elections, obtaining 31 of the 49 seats in the House of Assembly. In the 1997 elections, the party strengthened its dominance by gaining 35 of the 40 seats. In the 2002 elections, the PLP regained power, but the FNM swept the PLP out again in 2007. In 2012, the PLP won a resounding victory, and its leader, Perry Christie, took over as prime minister from the FNM's Hubert Ingraham.

The Bahamas began to recover from a protracted period of poor growth and heavy debt in 2013, after deferring fiscal consolidation and tax hikes in order to boost recovery. According to the International Monetary Fund, the economy swiftly stopped again, with gross domestic product (GDP) flatlining in 2013, declining in 2014–15, and rising just modestly in 2016. Nonetheless, by establishing the National Health Insurance (NHI) program in 2016, the government made a step toward fully implementing affordable universal health care coverage. Meanwhile, allegations of corruption have followed several delays in the inauguration of Baha Mar, the $4.2 billion Chinese-funded "mega resort" that was expected to boost the economy.

In The may 2017, the people reacted favorably to the FNM's commitment to promote Bahamian economic ownership by handing the opposition party a landslide win in the House of Assembly elections. Hubert Minnis was elected Prime Minister after the FNM won 35 seats to the PLP's four. Christie was not even re-elected to the position he had held for over four decades.

When Storm Dorian, a category 5 hurricane, hit the Bahamas in early September 2019, it wreaked havoc on Abaco, the other Abacos islands and cays, and Grand Bahama Island. "One of the greatest national crises in our country's history," Minnis said. As a result of the natural catastrophe, which caused losses estimated at $3.4 billion, at least 74 Bahamians died and more than 200 more were remained missing a year later.

When the coronavirus SARS-CoV-2 worldwide pandemic hit the Bahamas in 2020, it wreaked havoc on the tourism-dependent economy. When Minnis scheduled a snap election for September 2021, the government's handling of the public health crisis was a major campaign theme (by which time more than 500 Bahamians had died of causes related to COVID-19, the disease brought on by the virus). The people rejected Minnis' ambition to be the first Bahamian prime minister to be re-elected in more than two decades, giving a landslide win to the PLP, whose leader, Philip Davis, was elected prime minister.

New Providence Islands

A strange combination of opulent casinos and quiet shaded alleyways, splashy megaresorts and little communities that harken back to a bygone era, land development unequaled everywhere in the Bahamas, and enormous swaths of undeveloped land. New Providence Island is a throw-away destination. Two-thirds of Bahamians live on the island, which offers fast-paced lifestyle, nightlife that lasts until daybreak, and high-end retail areas. When the rush and bustle gets too much, there are plenty of peaceful stretches of sandy white beach where the only sound is the breaking waves.

Lawless pirates, Spanish conquerors, slave-holding British Loyalists who left the United States after the Revolutionary War, Civil War–era Confederate blockade runners, and Prohibition rum-runners have all passed through the island's history. Nonetheless, England, which dispatched its first royal governor to the island in

1718, continues to have the greatest impact on New Providence. Despite the fact that the Bahamas gained government power in 1967 and independence six years later, British influence continues to be felt.

Nassau serves as the country's capital, transportation hub, and financial and commercial center. The fortunate mix of tourist-friendly businesses, tropical weather, and island character with a European twist hasn't gone unnoticed: over 2.5 million cruise ship passengers visit Nassau's Prince George Wharf each year.

This capital city has a distinct hustling and bustling that you won't find elsewhere in the country, but that doesn't mean you have to join in. Active hobbies abound in New Providence, from shark diving and snorkeling to bicycle excursions, horseback riding, tennis, and golf. Paddleboarding, sailing, kayaking, and deep-sea fishing are just a few of the options available to avid water-sports enthusiasts. Alternatively, for a day excursion or an evening ride, simply cruise the pristine Bahamian seas.

Nassau Paradise Island

The Orientation

Paradise Island is located in the northern / central Bahamas, right off the north shore of New Providence Island. It's just a few minutes from Nassau's main city, and it's a little island on maps, measuring around 6 kilometres / 4 miles broad and barely 800 meters / 2,625 feet deep. Two bridges link the island to the mainland. The major lure of Paradise Island is its beaches, which are located in the north of the island and face the Atlantic Ocean. The Cabbage and Paradise beaches are flanked by hotels and stores, while the docks, marinas, and bridges are on the south side. The Paradise Island Golf Course is located in the east of the island, where it is the most lush, and out to the west, where the island narrows to a point, are more secluded beaches. The golf course is connected by Paradise Island Drive.

The Atlantis Bridge connects Nassau with the island's main road and leads to a center roundabout, which is a notable landmark. The large hotels that Paradise Island is known for are located to the north and west of this location. On maps, Paradise Lake lies immediately west of the roundabout, while the Dolphin Centre and dock are immediately south. Hotels in this area are practically like tiny towns, with their own beach, shops, and entertainment.

The old downtown section of Nassau is about 10 blocks long and four blocks wide, and it faces north toward the harbourfront. The high Prospect Ridge and Blue Hill Heights give prominent observation points to the south, and the primary residential area is located between these peaks. Bay Street connects the Atlantis Bridge to Paradise Island and serves as Nassau's principal east-west road.

Useful distances from Paradise Island:

- Adelaide Village 25 km / 15 miles (30 minutes, south-west)
- Blue Lagoon Island (boat) 5 km / 3 miles (30 minutes, north-east)
- Cable beach Golf Course 4 km / 3 miles (ten minutes, south-west)
- Lynden Pindling International Airport 20 km / 12 miles (30 minutes, south-west)
- Nassau 5 km / 3 miles (15 minutes, south)

Nassau History Overview

Nassau, the island's capital and biggest city, presently houses just under three-quarters of all Bahamas citizens. The Lynden Pindling

International Airport, which is located on the island of New Providence, is the Bahamas' largest airport.

The busy port and intriguing architecture of the city are among the first things most tourists to the Bahamas will notice during their time here. The alluring Paradise Island and its vast Atlantis resort are located exactly north-east of New Providence Island, and hence Nassau.

Settlement by the Spanish

Nassau's history has historically centred around its natural harbor, which has shielded the region from possible assaults and invasions, as well as the countless pirates, rum smugglers, freed slaves, and other individuals who have sought sanctuary here throughout the ages.

After Christopher Columbus arrived on the island he called San Salvador in 1492, the Lucayans, the area's first known inhabitants, were rapidly pushed out. The Spaniards, on the other hand, elected not to remain in Nassau for long, having been disappointed by the apparent paucity of gold on the island, which was not what they had anticipated.

Charles Town

Both the Bahamas and the Carolinas were claimed by England in 1629 by King Charles I. However, it wasn't until nearly two decades later that the Bahamas saw its first permanent English residents, when seasoned explorer William Sayles built a tiny and very formal town on adjacent Eleuthera Island. Nassau's history dates back to 1666, when it was established as Charles Town before gaining its present name in 1695.

Republic of Privateers

Present-day The early visitors to Nassau were far from religious, plundering the countless shipwrecks that dot the shore of the newly created city. After England issued a 'Letter of Marque' allowing privateers to attack any enemy vessel, the city became an unofficial privateer's republic. Blackbeard, the legendary pirate leader, was the local magistrate, and he was only one of many pirates that based themselves in the city throughout the 17th century. The privateers became criminals once the conflicts between England and other nations ended, and they were finally escorted off the Bahamas by warships.

Refuge for Loyalists and Slaves

Following the American Revolution, Nassau became a haven for a number of Loyalists, many of whom brought their slaves with them. When England made slave trafficking illegal in 1807, the Royal Navy seized several slave ships, resulting in the unwitting passengers gaining their freedom. The city's Over-the-Hill neighborhood was where the liberated slaves initially lived, and the bulk of the Bahamas' people are descendants of these West Africans.

Prohibition and Privateering

During the American Civil War, Nassau, along with the rest of the Bahamas, elected to defy the Union blockade by continuing to trade with Confederate states (1861 to 1865). During the notorious prohibition years, the Bahamas disobeyed American law once again by smuggling alcohol into southern ports. After King Edward VIII abdicated the monarchy, he and his divorced American socialite wife, Wallis Simpson, elected to reside in Nassau, ushering in a new period in the island's history and the start of a flourishing tourist sector. It's worth noting that the Bahamas just gained independence in 1973.

With the development of tourism, especially package vacations for Americans visiting the Caribbean, Nassau's fortunes skyrocketed. The massive construction of Atlantis, a half-billion-dollar themed hotel resort conceived by South African hotel mogul Sol Kerzner (of Sun City fame), has contributed significantly to Nassau's recent history. Its position on Paradise Island, just north of the cruise ship quayside, has given the Bahamas' capital an unquestionable appearance of refinement.

Best Traveling Period and the Climate Information

Islands Bahamas have a tropical marine climate with mild temperatures for the most of the year. Nassau's daytime temperatures are generally over 30°C / 86°F, while the Gulf Stream's flowing warm waters keep the water temperature reasonable all year. The Bahamas, like the rest of the Caribbean and Gulf States, is vulnerable to high humidity and rainfall, as well as a hurricane season in the summer. Winter is the greatest season to visit the Bahamas because of the weather. Everyone else, notably those from the northern US states and the upper Eastern Seaboard, generally arrives around this time. This time of year, it is dry and warm, but it also cools down wonderfully at night.

Climate Variations by Season / When to Visit

Because Nassau and Paradise Island are tropical, they do not have typical seasons like as spring, summer, autumn, or winter; instead, they are cooler, wetter, and wetter. With high daytime temperatures, moderate humidity, and minimal rainfall, the cool climate from December to April provides the best weather. Storms are unlikely, and the air is crisp and clear, with blue sky. December, January, and February are the busiest months, with March and April being significantly less expensive. The summer (wet and hot) months of the Bahamas are hurricane season, which lasts generally from June to November. Storms and hurricanes are most likely in the latter half of this period, particularly in August, September, and October, while inclement weather may strike at any moment beginning in May, when the rainy season officially begins. This is the low season, when hotel rooms are less expensive.

Hotels and Lodging

Paradise Island, located off the northern coast of Nassau, boasts the most costly lodging in the Bahamas. There are mega-luxury hotels and resorts here, such as Atlantis, where a night's stay in the Royal Towers may cost thousands of dollars. In this part of the world, you won't find any affordable, family-run guest rooms or comparable lodging. The enormous resort complexes of Paradise Island often offer all-inclusive packages, which include food, drink, and entertainment. You'll even get your own private beach. Although this is not for everyone, you can relax knowing that everything is taken care of. Summer offers better hotel rates, and lodging in downtown Nassau is often less expensive than comparable hotels on Paradise Island and near Cable Beach.

Where Should You Stay?

Atlantis is the biggest resort on Paradise Island, covering the majority of the populated area. Atlantis reigns supreme over Cabbage Beach in the center, as well as the beaches to the south, east, and west. There's a casino here, as well as fantastic lodging, shopping, and eating options. The One&Only Ocean Club is the second main resort on Paradise Island, located farther east. It's been around for decades and has a beautiful length of beach as well as a golf course. This resort was featured in a scene from the 2006 James Bond film Casino Royale, starring Daniel Craig, and it is usually seen to be more laid-back and less suffocating than Atlantis. A notable free attraction in this area is the Versailles Gardens and French Cloister.

The Sheraton Cable Beach Resort and Casino is located on West Bay Street in Nassau.

Other notable Paradise Island hotel resorts include the Riu Paradise Island, which has a long stretch of sandy beach adjacent to Atlantis, the Sunrise Beach Club and Villas, which are privately owned, and Comfort Suites, which is one of the more affordable options and provides free access to Atlantis. If you can't afford to stay at one of the Paradise Island hotels, go between April and November. Although you won't receive large savings on accommodations, rates may decrease by 20 or 30 percent during hurricane season. Alternatively, you may stay in a tiny guest house downtown Nassau, with decent options around Market Street, Bay Street, and Charlotte Street, all of which are near to Arawak Cay and Junkanoo Beach.

Transportation and Car Rental

On Paradise Island, there is no airport; the closest is on New Providence, near Lake Killarney and 16 kilometers (10 miles) west of Nassau. Flights from the United States and Europe land at Lynden Pindling Airport, and connections are simple to organize. There is no train service or regular bus service to Paradise Island, thus the only way to get here is via taxi or hotel shuttle.

Two bridges link the islands of Nassau and Paradise. Mackey Street goes to the Island Bridge from the city, whereas East Bay Street / Church Street links to the Atlantis Bridge. The bridges are also walkable, and the island is small enough to navigate on foot. Taxis are widely used on both islands, but minibuses provide a cost-effective alternative to taxis and link the major points of interest in Nassau, such as Cable Beach, Lyford Cay, and Sandy Point.

Arriving by air: Lynden Pindling International Airport (NAS) Lynden Pindling International Airport, formerly Nassau International Airport, is situated west of the capital and just south of both Gambier Village and Orange Hill Beach, where it gets direct flights from the United States and Europe. There is no bus service to Paradise Island, and the airport is fairly tiny with mediocre amenities and shops. Your hotel will normally offer a shuttle service for transfers, or if that is not possible, pricey meter-taxi transportation is available immediately outside the arrivals lounge. When traveling to major places such as Cable Beach and the Prince George Wharf, taxis usually provide set fares. (*Address: Coral Harbour Road*

/ Windsor Field Road, AP 59222, Nassau, New Providence, Bahamas, West Indies
Tel: +1 242 377 7281)

Car Service: All of the major rental businesses, including Avis, Budget, Dollar, and Hertz, have offices at Lynden Pindling International Airport, as well as a number of local companies that rent scooters in Nassau on Festival Place, the Prince George Wharf, and West Bay Street. Because Paradise Island is a tiny, heavily inhabited island, a rental vehicle is not required unless you wish to go throughout New Providence. Car rentals may be pre-booked online and picked up at the airport, or you can just get a vehicle from a rental agency at the hotel. It's worth noting that this island has a small access fee.

Buses and Coaches: Visitors may move throughout New Providence by bus, with minibuses (jitneys) and hotel shuttles replacing taxis as the primary mode of transportation. These minibuses run between the hours of 6:00 and 20:00, albeit they do not adhere to any specific timetable. Downtown buses run along Bay and Frederick Streets, with several bus stations strewn across the city and beyond, however you may ask the driver to stop anywhere you choose. Buses do not cross the bridges into Paradise Island, but instead stay on New Providence.

Taxis, boats, and ferries: For the most part, you can move about Paradise Island on foot, while taxis are available for journeys around the island, as well as to and from Nassau and the airport. Taxis are metered and tend to congregate around the major hotels and tourist sites. Taxis and limousines may be rented by the hour for tours around the island and New Providence. However, the costs are rather high. Every 30 minutes, water taxis run between Nassau's Prince George Wharf and the Paradise Island Ferry Terminal (south). The dock is situated on Casino Drive, and services are available between the hours of 9:00 a.m. and 18:00 p.m. This brief trek takes around 10 minutes to complete.

Nassau International Airport

The principal entrance to the Bahamas archipelago is the Nassau Lynden Pindling International Airport (also known as the Bahamas Nassau International Airport). It is located in Nassau, the Bahamas' capital, and New Providence Island. The national flag carrier, Bahamasair, is situated here, and the hub is also serviced by a number of international airlines, including British Airways and Continental Airlines. The airport, which has two terminals and two runways, is located on the western side of New Providence Island, not far from the major beach resorts of Paradise Island. The majority of flights come here from the surrounding US mainland (American Airlines) and Canada (Air Canada), with a direct trip from London provided by British Airways. Although the venue is generally well-equipped, ground transportation is limited.

When it was named as Windsor Field, the Nassau Lynden Pindling International Airport played an essential role during WWII. It now has a three-million-passenger capacity, and its main runway can handle A380 aircraft. The Lookout There, an onsite observation platform, is available. Nassau Lynden Pindling International Airport is 16 kilometers (10 miles) west of the city and a short distance from Paradise Island. A and B are the names of the two terminals. International (non-US) and domestic flights are served by Terminal A, while US and domestic flights are served by Terminal B. (*Address: Coral*

Harbour Road / Windsor Field Road, AP 59222, Nassau, New Providence, Bahamas, West Indies, Tel: +1 242 377 7281)

Facilities:

- Currency exchange in either terminal and the Royal Bank of Canada in Terminal A.
- ATMs in both terminals.
- Good eating and drinking, including the Bahama Dutch Oven, the Heineken Lounge, Bootleggers Bar and Dunkin' Donuts.
- Mainly souvenir shops including Caribbean Lighthouse, along with duty free goods and a newsagent (Cays News).
- Car hire companies include Avis, Budget, Hertz, Thrifty and Dollar.
- Business services are available at the nearby Radisson and Wyndham resorts.

- Adapted toilets, ramps, telephones and reserved parking spaces for disabled visitors.
- Three car parks, with short-stay and long-term parking options.

Cars, buses, taxis, and limousines: The JFK Drive and the Tonique Williams-Darling Highway connect Nassau to the Nassau Lynden Pindling International Airport, which is approximately a 20-minute drive away. Driving to Paradise Island from the airport is also simple, since it circumnavigates Nassau and connects with West Bay Street. In the Bahamas, traffic is driven on the left side of the road. While there are no public buses that serve the airport, the major hotels provide shuttle services. Your airport transfers will almost always be included if you book one of these hotels. It's worth noting that the bus ride to Paradise Island takes around 30 minutes. On both New Providence and Paradise islands, taxis are available to take you to your desired location. Taxis with fixed rates congregate at Arrivals, while metered taxis leave from the road outside the airport premises. Rich and Famous and A Touch of Class, two limousine companies established here, provide a more affluent option to get into Nassau and other places throughout the islands.

Tourism

Nassau, the Bahamas' capital and principal town on New Providence Island, is the throbbing heart of the Bahamas Islands, and it conceals a diverse range of fascinating things to do in Nassau Bahamas. With over 700 islands that make up the Bahamas archipelago, Nassau is an ideal starting point for seeing the Bahamas Out Islands, and Bahamas Air Tours offers Bahamas Day Trips by aircraft to the Exumas and Harbour Island, two of the most popular destinations. Beyond of the dazzling hotels and towering resorts in Nassau and Paradise Island, it's easy to overlook the rich history and culture that resides outside the gleaming hotels and towering resorts. Nassau is known for its rich history, culture, and food. There's no better way to learn about Bahamian culture than to take a look at our list of top things to do in Nassau, Bahamas, and see how many you can check off on your next Bahamas vacation!

The Bahamas' most populous island, New Providence, is home to more than 65 percent of the archipelago's total population. Nassau, the Bahamian capital and the main city in this tropical island chain, is situated on New Providence. Nassau, on the upper end of New Providence Island, sits immediately south of Paradise Island and bustles day and night. Old Bahamian architecture, museums, galleries, and stores are just a few of the sites to see here. Paradise Island is a lovely tiny island off New

Providence's north coast. It offers beautiful beaches and some of the most luxurious accommodations in the Bahamas. Here is where Atlantis, a five-star resort with every possible amenity, including a private beach, retail malls, and a glitzy casino, is located. On Paradise Island, tourism is huge, particularly in the winter when New Yorkers come to holiday.

Paradise Island is stunning and provides everything you could want from a vacation, including a golf course and a plethora of kid-friendly activities. While there is no official tourist information bureau, the hotels will provide you with all of the information you want. Alternatively, go to George Street in Nassau, where the Bahamas Ministry of Tourism is located. New Providence, like the rest of the Bahamas, is known for its beautiful beaches and silky white sand, with Cable Beach being one of the most popular and readily accessible from

Nassau. A variety of beachfront resorts are located here, and numerous water activities such as reef snorkeling and windsurfing are accessible. Cabbage Beach is one of the most popular beaches on Paradise Island, and it's a great area to go jet skiing, parasailing, or ride about in colorful inflatable banana boats.

You may experience the finest of both islands if you are willing to hop between New Providence and Paradise Island. In Nassau, you may take a variety of cruises and boat tours that stop at different sights along the route and include snorkeling, swimming, beach activities, and an all-inclusive BBQ lunch. The Ardastra Gardens, Zoo, and Conservation Centre is also in Nassau, and the hand-feeding of friendly lorikeets is a huge attraction. Much of the tourism on Paradise Island revolves on the massive Atlantic Casino resort, which has a facsimile of the 'Lost City of Atlantis' (dubbed 'The Dig') as well as an extensive water park featuring terrifying water slides including the Leap of Faith, the Serpent Slide, and the Abyss. The family-friendly Dolphin Cay, the beautiful Versailles Gardens, and the busy stores in the fairly costly Marina Village are all on Paradise Island.

Paradise Island is home to some of the region's most magnificent monuments, including the Atlantis Resort and the One&Only Ocean Club, which both provide plenty of unforgettable vistas. The French Cloister, which is situated inside the Versailles Gardens and dates from the 12th century, may be found there. Away from the more contemporary and glamorous beach resorts, the 18th-century Government House with its majestic pink and white Georgian front gives a touch of grandeur to Nassau. Parliament Square, which is a block away from the Commonwealth of the Bahamas Court of Appeal and houses the House of Assembly, the Public Library, the

Senate, and the Supreme Court, is close by and just off the Western Esplanade.

Despite the fact that most visitors come to the Bahamas for the sun, beach, and sea, Nassau has a number of cultural attractions. The Pirate Museum, situated in downtown Nassau, is one such site, offering intriguing facts on the Golden Age of Piracy, around 300 years ago, when this city drew the largest number of pirates in the whole New World. The Pompey Museum at Vendue House is another noteworthy cultural site, with displays chronicling the lives and journeys of Bahamian slaves. The National Art Gallery of the Bahamas has works by famous painters from the Bahamas and the Americas for those in need of a fine-art fix. The Junkanoo Mini-Museum, located near Cabbage Beach on Paradise Island, is well worth a visit and showcases native music, dancing, and 'Junkanoo' street processions.

Because the Bahamas has so much to offer, it's a good idea to go out and about by taking a ship or a short flight to nearby islands. The Blue Lagoon Island is particularly nearby, where natural beauty abounds and snorkeling is a popular pastime. Great Abaco is located to the north of Paradise Island and is known for its scuba diving. Other attractions on the island include Cherokee Sound, Hope Town, Marsh Harbour, Sandy Point, and Treasure Cay. Andros, Eleuthera, Great Exuma, and San Salvador are all within easy reach of Nassau, with beautiful beaches, an imposing church, and information about the period when daring explorer Christopher Columbus arrived here many years ago.

Things you can Do in Nassau Bahamas

1. Paradise Island

Paradise Island, the little sister of New Providence Island, is located close off the coast of Nassau. Paradise Island is readily accessible by car or boat, and is connected by two road bridges that rise into the Nassau skyline (frequent boat taxi service departs from downtown waterfront). Paradise Island is the place to go if you want to have a good time with your family. White sand beaches, the Aquaventure Waterpark, a casino, shopping arcade, conference center, and a golf course are all part of the huge Atlantis Bahamas resort. On Paradise Island, you'll find 5-star hotels like the Ocean Club, which was featured in the 2006 James Bond film Casino Royale.

2. Day Trips to Exuma

Visiting the Bahamas Swimming Pigs at Pig Beach (Big Major Cay) in the Exuma Cays archipelago is the number one activity to do in Nassau, Bahamas. Take an aircraft from Nassau to Exuma and travel to Swimming Pigs Island for the ultimate Exuma Excursion day excursion with Bahamas Air Tours. Swimming with sharks is also available at Compass Cay Marina in the Exuma Cays.

3. Junkanoo Beach

The nearest length of white sand to downtown and old town Nassau is Junkanoo Beach. It's a beautiful length of beach with swaying palm trees and tiki houses on each side. From the colorful tiki huts and booths, local merchants sell Bahamian food, beverages, and refreshments.

4. Parliament Square

The iconic Queen Victoria monument from 1905 stands boldly in front of Parliament Square, which was created in 1815. The Senate Buildings, which house the Supreme Court, are located behind the parliament (there are often prisoner vans delivering prisoners for trial).

5. Government House

Government House, the official house of the Governor General of the Bahamas, is a colonial symbol. On the stairs leading up to government house, a statue of Christopher Columbus is prominently displayed. Columbus was the first to find the Bahamas, which he dubbed Baha Mar. (Spanish for shallow waters).

6. Graycliff Heritage Village

The Graycliff Heritage, run by the Graycliff Hotel, runs along W Hill Street. Graycliff is home to the Bahamas Heritage Museum, which is another historic thing to do in Nassau (opened in 2014). The Graycliff Cigar Company, Graycliff Chocolatier, and Bahama Barrels wine tasting are all located on campus.

7. Cabbage Beach

Cabbage Beach is the longest length of white sand on Paradise Island, and it serves as the background for some of Nassau's most luxurious hotels, including the Atlantis Resort, Rio, and Four Seasons Ocean Club. The cabbages that supported this form of farming were named after the agricultural area that used to occupy Paradise Island (pig farming was originally nicknamed "Hog Island"). Waterskiing, jet skiing, snorkeling, and parasailing are just a few of the watersport activities available in Nassau, Bahamas.

8. Pompey Museum

Just off Pompey Square is the Pompey Museum of Slavery and Emancipation (between the downtown waterfront and bay street, adjacent to the Nassau Straw Market). The history of slavery in the Bahamas is documented in the Pompey Museum. The structure, which was once a market building, dates back to the 1760s. Pompey Museum, which is painted pink (as are other government buildings) and has a distinct history, is a fascinating activity to do in Nassau Bahamas.

9. Pirates of Nassau

Pirates of Nassau is the only interactive pirate experience in Nassau, transporting you back to 1716 and the period of piracy, making it one of the most thrilling things to do in Nassau Bahamas. With numerous informative displays and recreations, visitors may learn about the Golden Age of Piracy, which started in 1969 when privateer Henry Every took the ship the Fancy to Nassau and paid local authorities to create Nassau as a secure base for pirates to operate from. The Smugglers Restaurant is located next door in Nassau's Old Town, under the steeple of Christ Church Anglican Cathedral, on a very attractive street.

10. Heritage Museum of the Bahamas

The Heritage Museum of the Bahamas is situated in the Mountbatten House, a historical listed structure owned by the Graycliff estate. Hamilton White, a well-known British antiquities collector, owns the exhibits and collections. On your tour, take in the vibrant sceneries along W Hill Street and the remainder of Graycliff Heritage Village.

11. Queens Staircase

The Queen's Staircase is a 65-step staircase cut into the limestone cliffs. They were erected by salves in the 1790s. The stairway served as a means of escape from Fort Fincastle, which located atop the hill. A flowing waterfall and tropical flora surround the Queen's stairwell.

12. Fort Fincastle

Fort Fincastle gives well-deserved views over the skyline of New Providence Island and the Nassau Cruise Port for guests who climb the neighboring Queen's Staircase. Because all cruise ship trips stop here, this is one of the most popular things to do in Nassau, Bahamas. Lord Dunmore erected the Fort in 1793 to safeguard Nassau from pirates.

13. Blue Lagoon

Salt Cay, a little island off the coast of Paradise Island, is home to Blue Lagoon. To get to the private island, visitors take a picturesque boat journey from Nassau Harbour. It's consistently ranked as one of the best things to do in Nassau, Bahamas. Stingray encounters, Segway tours, Shark encounters, Beach days, sea lion encounters, and the top attraction, a dolphin encounter and swim, are just a few of the thrilling things available on the island.

14. John Watlings Distillery

Adults will like this as one of the finest things to do in Nassau, Bahamas! The Buena

Vista Estate's freshly renovated John Watlings distillery was featured in the James Bond film Casino Royale. Look for the signpost on the grounds' grass! The distillery of John Watling provides guided tours, a museum, and a bar where you can sample drinks and rum!

15. Bahamas National Art Gallery

The National Art Gallery of the Bahamas is housed on the grounds of Villa Doyle, a palace erected in the 1860s and was home to the Bahamas' first chief judge. The structure was restored for seven years before it reopened in 1996. The NAGB is a non-profit organization that collects, preserves, and displays historic and modern Bahamian art.

16. Downtown Waterfront

Woodes Rodgers Walk roadway extends through the Nassau Downtown Waterfront area. The major landing area for cruise ship tourists on day trips to Nassau, with wide harbour views of Nassau Port. Because of the high volume of tourists, the Waterfront area is lined with pubs and restaurants. Senor Frogs is the biggest of them all. The James Bond Never Say Never Bar & Grill, the Tropicana Bar, Lukka Kairi, Fat Tuesdays, and the Pirate Republic Brewing Company are all located here.

17. On Paradise Island, there is a French Cloister and Versailles Gardens.

The French Cloister is the centerpiece of the Versailles Gardens at Paradise Island. It is a remarkable 14th century Augustinian monastery that was disassembled and moved from Europe by William Randolph Hearst. The Four Seasons One & Only Ocean Club owns and manages the property, yet it may be seen from the public street.

18. Nassau Straw Market.

The Nassau Straw Market is a popular destination for souvenirs and is located in the heart of Bay Street and the Nassau Downtown Waterside region. Many local sellers with booths offering local handicrafts and souvenirs may be found here.

19. Atlantis Resort Aquaventure.

Aquaventure is the biggest waterpark in the Bahamas. On Paradise Island, inside the Atlantis Resort. Aquaventure is one of the most entertaining things to do in Nassau, Bahamas, and it is open to tourists who are not staying at the Atlantis. A day ticket that includes admission to the Cove Beach and swimming facilities may be purchased. There are several water slides, river rides, 20 swimming places, a children's play area, and 11 swimming pools in the waterpark.

20. The Hilton Colonial Hotel Beach.

The Hilton Colonial Hotel offers a huge outdoor swimming pool and restaurant and is the only downtown hotel with direct beach access. Day tourists from cruise ships flock to the beautiful sand beach.

21. Festival Place.

Festival Place is the major cruise port terminal, including an outdoor retail area where you can purchase souvenirs, plan day excursions and tours, and sample native Bahamian food. Although it is not one of the top things to do in Nassau, Bahamas, it is an intriguing site to visit even if you are not a cruise ship passenger!

22. Arawak Cay (Touristy Fish Fry).

Arawak Cay is a 20-minute walk from downtown Nassau, located at the end of Junkanoo Beach. It is known as the touristic fish fry, featuring high-end eateries such as the ever-popular Twin Brothers. For Bahamian Fish and Chips, this is the place to go!

23. Potters Cay (Local Fish Fry).

Potters Cay, located under the Paradise Island road bridges, is perhaps Nassau's best-kept secret. It's the locals' Fish Fry. Locals may be seen here sipping beers and drinks while eating conch salads and grilled seafood. If you want to sample real Bahamian cuisine, this is the place to go! Furthermore, the costs are far lower than those of any other restaurants in Nassau.

24. Clifton Heritage Park.

The Clifton Heritage, located on the extreme western coast of New Providence Island, is one of our favorite things to do in Nassau, Bahamas. It is home to a rare assemblage of historical and culturally significant sites in Nassau, covering 208 hectares of land. The Clifton Heritage Park is one of the top Nassau attractions, with a diversified ecology, caverns and nature walks, as well as a one-of-a-kind underwater sculpture park.

25. Cable Beach.

Cable Beach is a length of beautiful white sand that is home to some of Nassau's most opulent resorts and hotels; the Melia Nassau, Baha Mar, and Sandals Bahamian are all popular places to stay in Nassau. It is without a doubt one of Nassau's best beaches, named after a telephone wire that washed up on the coast here on New Providence Island.

26. The Primeval Forest.

The Primeval Forest, which is managed by the Bahamas National Trust, is a gorgeous natural wonderland. It's a 30-minute journey from downtown Nassau from this location on the western edge of New Providence (past the Airport). On top of limestone caverns and sink holes, a thick and magnificent tropical forest grows. Keep an eye out for the different animals that calls this place home!

<u>27. Rose Island.</u>

Rose Island is a popular day trip location for tourists. Unspoilt white sand beaches and tropical flora may be found on the long but narrow island nearest to Nassau and Paradise Island. It boasts some of Nassau's greatest snorkeling, making it one of the best things to do in Nassau.

Interesting Things to Do in Nassau

When you're planning a vacation to the Caribbean, you'll want to learn about the best things to see and do in Nassau, Bahamas. Nassau, the Bahamas' capital and the region's primary tourism center, provides travelers with everything from breathtaking landscape to urban pleasures.

However, as one of the Bahamas' 700 islands, New Providence (also known as Nassau) should be your starting point for seeing the rest of the country.

While visitors to the Bahamas may emphasize things to do in Atlantis Bahamas, the magnificent Exuma Islands, a lovely archipelago of 365 tropical islands, are some of the greatest places on the island. Even if they aren't as well-known, they are all definitely worth a visit! Today, we'll discuss some of the top things to do in Nassau, Bahamas. You'll want to keep reading to find out things to do in Nassau, Bahamas, from learning about local history to taking swimming with pigs excursions.

1. Lounge Around on the Nassau Beaches

Many visitors seeking for things to do in Nassau, Bahamas are mostly interested in one thing: beaches. The good news is that you've arrived to the perfect area if you're seeking for smooth, powdery white sand and water so clear you can see your feet in it!

Despite the fact that Nassau is not the largest island, it has over a dozen different and beautiful beaches. Some are free and open to the public, while others are owned by hotels. Cabbage Beach, Junkanoo Beach, Cable Beach, and Love Beach are all postcard-perfect stretches that even the most discerning visitors can't resist. Don't be scared to visit them all if you have the time; beach hopping is one of the finest things to do in Nassau, Bahamas!

2. Visit Hilton Colonial Hotel Beach

After visiting your first beach in Nassau, Bahamas, are you wondering what to do? Go to a different one! The Hilton Colonial Hotel, only a short walk from Junkanoo Beach, owns a beautiful length of beach that is a must-see attraction. It has blue sea, swaying palms, and the Caribbean ambiance that visitors love, much like the other of Nassau's beaches. Because this is a private beach, you must purchase a day admission. You will, however, be allowed to enjoy the beach, swimming pool, and hotel restaurant after you have done so.

3. Push Your Limits at the Atlantis Aquaventure Waterpark

A trip to Aquaventure Waterpark at Atlantis is another excellent thing to do in Nassau if you're looking for some action and excitement. Aquaventure is a 141-acre water park on Paradise Island including waterslides, bathing areas, refreshing pools, and lazy rivers. There are many more wonderful things to do in Atlantis Bahamas besides sliding down waterslides and getting that adrenaline rush you've been yearning. Make time on your Bahamas trip to visit Atlantis, from touring the park's beautiful, tropical gardens to renting a cabana on one of the exclusive beaches.

4. Embark on Exuma Day Trips

If you're ever unsure what to do in Nassau, Bahamas, keep in mind that the nearby islands are also easily accessible. Unfortunately, boat voyages may take many hours, which is why Bahamas Air Tours recommends doing Bahamas day vacations by air. You get unmatched views of the nation from the skies in a luxurious, private class jet, in addition to getting there in a fraction of the time.

The Exuma pigs, which are one of the most famous sights in the Bahamas, may be seen on a trip to the Exumas. You'll be able to view and touch them as they swim alongside you if you fly with any airline or use Bahamas Air Tours to get to the location. A day excursion with Bahamas Air Tours will enable you to swim with nurse sharks at Compass Cay, walk about Bitter Island Cay with iguanas, rest on the sand bars at Pipe Creek, and much more.

5. Get a Taste of History at Fort Fincastle

Are you curious in the history of the area? If you are, make a point of visiting Fort Fincastle, which is one of the greatest things to do in Nassau Bahamas. The British erected this 18th-century fort in downtown Nassau in an effort to discourage pirates from invading adjacent communities. Fort Fincastle is the ideal destination to learn about the island's history, from trekking up Queen's Staircase to seeing the fort's huge walls and cannons. The summit of the hill also has a beautiful view over the island, making it a popular site for photos. Fort Fincastle was named after Lord Dunmore's second title, Viscount Fincastle, the colonial governor who built the fort. It also operated as a lighthouse until

1817, when it was replaced with a lighthouse on Paradise Island.

6. Enjoy a Drink at John Watling's Distillery

Apart from the beaches, many visitors seeking for the best things to do in Nassau also want to know where they can have a drink. While there are plenty of martini bars and expensive restaurants to choose from, a visit to John Watling's Distillery is a must. The distillery, which is located on the ancient Buena Vista Estate, is one of the greatest things to do in Nassau Bahamas since it appeals to both history and rum enthusiasts. The guided walk of the grounds will appeal to history enthusiasts, while the rum tasting experience will appeal to rum fans (and anybody who appreciates a tasty drink). Just remember to bring your camera if you have one, since the grounds provide for great photo opportunities!

7. Stop by the Government House & the Columbus Statue

The Nassau Government House is the place to go if you want to learn more about the local government. The Governor General of the Bahamas is housed on a lovely ten-acre estate atop Mount Fitzwilliam. The Government House is both a political and a historical site. It was built in 1801, and it has a mix of American Colonial and Bahamian British architecture, making it one of the greatest things to do in Nassau Bahamas. A statue of Christopher Columbus may also be seen in front of the structure.

8. Visit the French Cloisters

Make time to see the French Cloisters and Versailles Gardens while enjoying the local architecture. The site of a 14th-century monastery at Montréjeau, France, is located on adjacent Paradise Island. Despite their origins in the Old World, they were purchased and constructed piece by piece on their current island location by an American businessman. You won't be allowed to go around the Cloisters unless you stay in the Four Seasons Ocean Club. However, a glimpse of them from the street is still possible!

The following are some of the best things to do in Nassau, Bahamas: While many people question what the best activities to do in Nassau are, maybe this article will help you plan ahead. Bring sunscreen, a camera, and a spirit of adventure; they will come in helpful when exploring the island! If you want to be informed about the activities and seasonal trip to Nassau be active with online vocational news from any of Bahamas website, online information gives you the accurate and timely information on Nassau and its environment. You will also have number of vocational services from various companies with formidable traveling offers.

Top Things to See in Nassau Bahamas

Are you looking for a lovely yet easily accessible holiday spot? If you are, Nassau is the place to be. There are so many things to visit in Nassau, Bahamas, with near-perfect weather and, of course, stunning beaches. Many visitors to the Bahamas, however, miss out on some of the many fun activities to do in Nassau and around the archipelago. Too many tourists leave without seeing a fort, taking a rum tour, or swimming with wild pigs. To help you make the most of your travel time and take advantage of the greatest things to see and do in Nassau, we've compiled a list of some of the must-see attractions. Everything included below is certainly worth a look, and in some situations, it may even be worth a second look.

Nassau, previously known as New Providence Island, is the Bahamas' capital.

Paradise Island, off its northern border, is home to the world-famous Atlantis Resort. Most people will either vacation in Nassau or transit through it since it is one of the major centers of the Bahamas. Nassau Port, being one of the busiest cruise ship ports in the world, delivers a large number of people to Downtown Nassau every day. As a result, Nassau has become the primary tourist destination in the Bahamas.

1. Paradise Island's Atlantis Resort.

As one of the top ranked things to visit in Nassau Bahamas, the world-famous park of Atlantis, located on Paradise Island, provides something for everyone. You may visit the luxury resort, aquarium, entertainment complex, or water park depending on your schedule. It's up to you to decide what to do in Atlantis Bahamas. The enormous outdoor aquarium, for example, will appeal to animal enthusiasts, since it has local tropical species. Many of the aquarium's tanks have Atlantis sculptures and ruins, so visiting the aquarium is a great chance to view some of the park's most beautiful sights.

You'll feel right at home in Atlantis Bahamas' water park, Aquaventure, if you're looking for fun things to do. The park has a leisurely river, but it also has water slides that would make even the bravest of hearts skip a beat. For example, the Leap of Faith sends you down an 18-foot slide while passing through a shark-infested lagoon.

2. Paradise Island's Cabbage Beach.

If we didn't include at least one stunning beach on our list, we'd be negligent. Cabbage Beach wins the honor for having crystal pure water and sand that is so white it looks like snow. This world-class beach is the place to go if you want to be a beach bum. It is one of New

Providence Island's nicest beaches, and it must be seen to be appreciated.

In addition to sunscreen and a beach towel, you may wish to carry snorkeling equipment. Just offshore, schools of tropical fish swim about, giving you a glimpse of the aquatic fauna that the Bahamas are known for. If you're feeling daring, you can even try paragliding or water skiing. Otherwise, there's nothing wrong with renting an umbrella for the day. Cabbage Beach, on Paradise Island, is easily accessible by taxi or boat. You may also stroll there from the port precinct in Nassau!

3. A day trip from Nassau to Exuma includes swimming with pigs.

When you're ready to get out of Nassau for a while, a day excursion from Nassau to Exuma might be exactly what you need. In addition to stunning landscape, an Exuma day trip includes a visit to Pig Beach, where you may see the world-famous swimming pigs. While it's vital to treat the pigs on Pig Island with care, they're exceedingly friendly and will willingly allow you to touch and stroke them while they play in the water beside you.

However, swimming pig excursions aren't the only thing you'll be able to do. Swim with sharks at Compass Cay, explore an underwater aircraft wreck, hang out with iguanas on Bitter Island Cay, and bury your toes into powder-soft sand bars at Pipe Creek on Exuma day tours with Bahamas Air Tours. All of this combines to make a journey to Exuma one of the best Bahamas day excursions by aircraft and a must-do adventure!

4. On Paradise Island, French Cloisters.

Many tourists to Nassau are surprised to see medieval-style cloisters that contrast sharply with the colonial-era buildings surrounding them. These aren't native to the island; they're from a

14th-century French convent, as you would expect. The remains were disassembled in the 1960s, transported to the island, and then rebuilt on a hill. Today, they allow you to inhale the sea wind and see a scene that harkens back to a bygone era. The cloisters and the adjoining Versailles-inspired garden are owned by the Four Seasons Ocean Club Resort. Even if you are not staying there, you can see them from the street.

5. Downtown Nassau's Fort Fincastle.

Fort Fincastle is a must-see for history fans seeking for things to do in Nassau, Bahamas. Fort Fincastle, built by Lord Dunmore in 1793, was one of numerous British initiatives to combat piracy in the area. The enormous guns and walls of the fort serve as a reminder of the gravity of the pirate threat. You'll get a spectacular view of the island after you reach the top of the fort.

6. The Queen's Staircase.

You'll ultimately find yourself at the foot of Queen's Staircase when you tour the Fort Fincastle Historic Complex. Hundreds of slaves carved the stairway into solid limestone in the 1790s as an emergency escape route from the fort above. Queen Victoria, the queen who controlled the British Empire for most of the nineteenth century, is honored by the current name. If you're seeking for picture opportunities, Queen's Staircase is the place to go. The site, which is surrounded by thick flora, is the ideal location for showing all your friends and family one of the best things to see in Nassau, Bahamas.

7. Parliament Square in Nassau's downtown area.

The Senate and the House of Assembly are housed in the pink buildings that beautify Parliament Square, which were built by loyalists (American colonists who backed the British Crown) in 1815. Within those walls, key discussions and choices about the Bahamas' future are held. If you're interested in politics, you'll be pleased to learn that you may listen in on the legislative process while the House is in session. Parliament Square is a good trip even if you're visiting the Bahamas to forget about politics. Aside from the colorful houses, there is a stunning monument of Queen Victoria and other picture opportunities.

8. John Watling's Distillery.

Without a drink (or many glasses) of rum, no journey to the Caribbean is complete. If you're seeking for additional things to do in Nassau, Bahamas, stopping by John Watling's Distillery for a drink is always a good idea. John Watling's Distillery, once the Buena Vista Estate, is now Nassau's top rum sampling location. You may also take guided excursions throughout the estate, which are available due to the site's vast history. The distillery is the spot to utilize your expensive camera if you have one. Even the most visually aware Instagram accounts would benefit from the building's vivid red, white, and blue hues.

Social Tour of Nassau

Nassau, the Bahamas' capital, is a busy metropolis of marketplaces, street sellers, and shopping arcades, in stark contrast to the Bahamas' isolated coves and vast lengths of unspoilt beach. You'll spend a morning or afternoon with a driver and guide touring the city on this small group trip.

For views of the city and the whole of New Providence Island, start with Fort Charlotte, an 18th-century stone fort that defends Nassau Harbour. Then you'll go into the city proper, where you'll see the city's vividly painted Georgian buildings, including the pastel-pink

Parliament House and the ornate colonnades of Government House.

Then it's a quick trip to Bay Street in Nassau to see a straw market. Straw weaving was traditionally used to make fishing traps and baskets, but today the crowded market focuses on more attractive straw crafts, and there's still time to pick up some hand-crafted mementos if you want to.

Your driver and guide will pick you up from your accommodation and transport you to Fort Charlotte, where your tour will begin. It was never utilized, which is fortunate given that the location was constructed such that the barracks would be in direct line of fire from the fort's own guns. You may take a walk inside the dungeons, moat, and subterranean passages, as well as ascend to the top of the barracks for panoramic views of the city.

After there, it's a short drive down to center Nassau, where you can see the city's Georgian architecture. The pink Parliament Square buildings with their brilliant green shutters, as well as the Parliament Building, are visible. The Parliament Building is fronted by a huge statue of Queen Victoria. There's also the chance to see Government House, which is currently the home of the Bahamas' Governor-General and sits majestically atop Mount Fitzwilliam.

You'll next see an old colonial prison and Gregory's Arch, a simple stone arch erected in 1849 to divide Nassau's largely European metropolis from Grant's Town, a population of once enslaved Africans. Finally, you'll visit the Nassau Straw Market in downtown Nassau. While it used to be a place where fisherman got their straw traps and baskets, it's now a display for a more intricate kind of straw craft. Handwoven straw products, such as slippers, backpacks, and caps, are on display at the densely packed kiosks. If you want to do some buying, your guide can explain how the craft has evolved and recommend some of the finest shops.

Favourite Attractions

Tourist Attractions

The huge Atlantis Resort and the One&Only Ocean Club, located farther east, absorb a large portion of Paradise Island. These colossi have their own beaches and side tourism attractions, and they're all within easy driving distance of Nassau, with Atlantis being the most well-equipped. The Atlantis Resort has a major water park, as well as an aquarium and retail centers. The One&Only Ocean Club, meantime, boasts the famed Versailles Gardens, while the several beaches near Nassau and Paradise Island are popular with vacationers, with Cabbage Beach and Paradise Beach being particularly popular.

Atlantis Resort

On Paradise Island, the Atlantis Resort is the primary attraction and landmark. This all-encompassing resort, located in the heart of Cabbage Beach, has a hotel, casino, water park, nightclub, theatre, comedy club, and a slew of other activities (see below). One of the park's water slides even sends guests directly past a shark tank. There are also retail centers, restaurants, and pubs. If you are not staying here, you will need to purchase a costly permit to enter Atlantis. The Beach Tower, Coral Towers, Cove Atlantis, Harbourside Resort, and Royal Towers are among the resort's accommodations, with the Bridge Suite connecting two towers and comfortably ranking among the world's most costly hotel suites. (*Address: Casino Drive,*

Paradise Island, Bahamas, BS) Tel: +1 242 363 3000.

Open hours: daily 24 hours

Admission: charge

Atlantis Casino

This massive resort has a fantastic casino, the largest in the Bahamas. There are rows of slot machines, a plethora of gaming tables (baccarat, blackjack, Caribbean stud poker, craps, and roulette), as well as a range of restaurants and performances. The Atlantis Paradise Island Casino, which is mostly deserted during the day, soon fills up at night. Poolside gaming is provided in a special outdoor pavilion at the 'Cain at the Cove' location, which is ideal for visitors searching for a unique casino vacation experience. Every year, the casino hosts a number of competitions and gambling-related events. (*Address: Casino Drive, Paradise Island, Bahamas, BS*)

Tel: +1 242 285 2684. Open hours: daily 10:00 to 04:00. Admission: charge to enter Atlantis

The Dig, Atlantis

The Dig, situated under the Royal Towers hotel complex and supposedly the world's largest open-air aquatic exhibit, is part of the Atlantis Resort and is one of the major sites on Paradise Island. It's a full-scale recreation of the legendary 'Lost City of Atlantis,' replete with tunnels and aquatic life. Sharks, jellyfish, and large manta rays may be found in the enormous aquariums, pools, and lagoons. The location also contains waterfalls and is well-designed, with rubble and crumbling constructions meant to symbolize this legendary city. (*Address: Royal Towers, 1 Casino Drive, Paradise Island, Bahamas, BS*). Tel: +1 242 363 3000

Open hours: daily. Admission: charge

Dolphin Cay, Atlantis

The popular Dolphin Cay attraction is located on the southern edge of Paradise Island, opposite Paradise Lake. This dolphin habitat, which also houses sea lions and manta rays, is one of the world's largest and greatest, with visitors having the opportunity to learn about the creatures and even swim with them. Various trips and activities are provided in both the shallows and the deep. Sessions are usually two hours long. (*Address: Paradise Beach Drive, Paradise Island, Bahamas, BS*). Open hours: daily 08:30 to 16:00. Admission: charge

Versailles Gardens

The Versailles Gardens and the French Cloister are both located on Paradise Island in this lovely location. They are part of the One&Only Ocean Club and are located in the island's center. They provide a nice break from the beach or when it becomes too hot and you need a nice shaded location to unwind. The gardens are well-kept and located around a 15-minute walk from Cabbage Beach's main length. (*Address: One&Only Ocean Club, Ocean Club Drive, Paradise Island, Bahamas, BS*). Tel: +1 242 302 2000. Open hours: daily 24 hours Admission: free

Potter's Cay Market

Potter's Cay is a bustling seafood market located under the Paradise Island Exit Bridge, near to the Bahamas Ferries pier, and a short walk from the Canadian Embassy, where you may sample fresh fish and conch. Many residents come here just after the boats arrive to buy fish from the wooden booths, which is as fresh as it gets. The lovely conch shells may also be purchased as souvenirs. Boat tours depart from this location and include a range of cruise packages. Of note, this area is best avoided at night. Open hours: daily | Admission: free

Marina Village

Marina Village, a flashy shopping area near to Atlantis on Paradise Island, with pastel-colored residences and over 20 retail businesses. This famous attraction was designed to look like Bay Street in Nassau, Bahamas. Many people just window shop since it is so pricey, especially when Nassau stores sell the same products for considerably less. The Marina Village has three major plazas, a variety of restaurants, some with live Caribbean entertainment, and a lot of charm. Fashion, beachwear, and handcrafted crafts, as well as elegant cafés and restaurants, come to mind. Open hours: daily | Admission: free. Address: Marina Village, Paradise Island, Bahamas, BS

Paradise Island Golf Course / Ocean Club

The Paradise Island Golf Course is a decent course, albeit not quite as nice as the

adjacent Cable Beach Golf Club on New Providence. It's well-kept and follows the shore along the eastern portion of the island, with fairways and greens that overlook the water. Golf instruction, equipment rental, and a fancy 19th hole are all offered. Those who stay at the Sun International Hotel will be given priority when it comes to tee times. (*Address: Paradise Island Drive, Bahamas, BS*). Tel: +1 242 677 4175.
Open hours: daily 07:30 to dusk
Admission: charge

Ardastra Gardens, Zoo And Conservation Centre

Around 300 different animals call the Ardastra Gardens, Zoo, and Conservation Centre home, including various free-flying tropical birds, Madagascar lemurs, jaguars, terrapins, reptiles, and caiman crocodiles. The zoo was established in the 1930s and is most known for its friendly flock of West Indian flamingos, who are paraded about the grounds many times a day. Visitors to the farmyard section will be able to feed the beautifully colored lorikeets and macaw parrots, as well as touch the animals. For the younger guests, there is also a playground. (*Address: Chippingham Road, Nassau, Bahamas, BS*). Tel: +1 242 323 5806.

Open hours: daily 09:00 to 17:00

Admission: charge, discounts available for children, children aged under four years are free

Cruises And Boat Trips

New Providence has a variety of boat rides to select from, with the bulk of cruises leaving from the Woodes Rogers Walk or the Paradise Island Ferry Terminal, respectively. Cruises are a gorgeous and convenient way to see the coast, with some packages including reef snorkeling, BBQ lunches, and time on a quiet sandy beach, with stops at Harbour Island and Rose Island. The Seaworld Explorer, which seats just under 50 people, provides something a bit different and bills itself as a semi-submarine thanks to its underwater viewing section, where windows allow amazing views of the Sea Gardens Marine Park. Open hours: daily |hours vary according to operator |Admission: charge.

Tel: +1 242 363 1552 (America's Cup Sailing Adventure)
Tel: +1 242 323 2166 (Bahamas Ferries)
Tel: +1 242 363 4430 (Flying Cloud Catamaran Cruises)
Tel: +1 242 363 1466 (Powerboat Adventures)
Tel: +1 242 356 2548 (Seaworld Explorer)

Scuba Diving And Snorkelling

With shallow coral reefs and a number of colonized wrecks, there are some good snorkeling and diving options near to the coast. The greatest scuba diving places are usually located close off the south-westerly coast, between Lyford Cay and Coral Harbour. It is possible to dive among sharks and stingrays, as well as ride underwater scooters, if you are searching for a unique experience. Don't worry if you've never scuba dived before; a three-hour course will teach you the fundamentals, and most diving companies will pick you up from your hotel for free. | Open hours: daily | Admission: charge for equipment hire and tuition. Tel: +1 242 393 6054 (Bahama Divers). Tel: +1 242 362 4171 (Stuart Cove's Dive and Snorkel)

Beaches

Cable Beach is the main stretch of tropical white sand on New Providence, and it curls to the west of downtown Nassau. A wide range of water activities are available near Cable, including coral snorkeling, reef fishing, sailing, and windsurfing. A number of bustling, freshly renovated beachfront resorts call Wire Beach home, and it got its name when a telegraphic cable washed ashore here towards the end of the 19th century. The Nassau Beach Hotel, the Crystal Palace, the Sandals, the Sheraton Resort, and the Wyndham are just a few of the major hotels and resorts around Cable Beach.

On Paradise Island, there are a few beaches, with Cabbage Beach being the most popular, as it is located just in front of the Atlantis Resort. This is a lovely length of white sand with turquoise waves, however it is bordered in the middle by giant hotels. Water activities like as jet skiing and parasailing are offered at Cabbage Beach, as well as inflatable banana boat rides and snorkeling tours. Paradise Beach is located to the north-west and can only be accessed by boat or on foot. Colonial Beach may be found near the point of Paradise Island, if you continue west. Arawak and Smugglers Beaches are quieter beaches on the eastern edge.

Landmarks and Monuments

The One&Only Ocean Club and the Atlantis Resort share many of Nassau's and Paradise Island's most remarkable monuments and vistas. The breathtaking Versailles Gardens and French Cloister can be found at One&Only, which was featured in the latest James Bond film Casino Royale.

Marina Village, a retail district on the island, is an excellent place to see the pastel-colored buildings, while Parliament Square is home to some of Nassau's most recognized attractions. The Government House, with its exquisite candy pink construction, is quite a regal sight in the Prospect Ridge neighborhood.

French Cloister.

The French Cloister is part of the One&Only Ocean Club and is located inside the Versailles Gardens. Visitors are sometimes startled to find that this is a true cloister that was erected in southern France during the 12th century and was recently transported and reassembled here. However, the narrative does not end there; putting the cloister back together took a few of years since nothing had been labeled. While meandering around the grounds, the French Cloister is really lovely to contemplate. Daily hours of operation | Admission is free. +1 242 363 2501 (Address: One&Only Ocean Club, Ocean Club Drive, Paradise Island, Bahamas, BS)

Government House

The Government House, with its stately Georgian-style architecture, serves as the official house of the Governor General of the Bahamas and has been a significant local icon since it was built as a private estate in 1737. The property was acquired by the government in 1799, and the Governor General moved there shortly after. The

Government House has a high position above Hill Street and is easily identifiable due to its pink and white front, which is flanked by a large monument of Christopher Columbus. The entryway is particularly impressive, with a steep stairway, four elaborate columns, and a portico flanking it. Visitors are not permitted to enter the structure, although they are allowed to wander about the grounds. The changing of the guards event takes place on alternating Saturday mornings at 10:00 a.m. (*Address: Corner of Blue Hill Road and Duke Street, Nassau, Bahamas, BS*)

Tel: +1 242 322 1875. Open hours: daily grounds only

Admission: free

Parliament Square

Parliament Square is located on the east side of downtown Nassau, bordered by Bay Street to the north, East Street to the east, Shirley Street to the south, and Parliament Street to the west (west). Rawson Square, the Royal Victoria Gardens, and the Bambu Music Bar are all nearby, while the Supreme Court, the House of Assembly, the Senate, the Nassau Public Library and Museum, and Queen Victoria's Statue, as well as the Gardens of Remembrance, are all located on Parliament Square. (*Address: Parliament Square, Parliament Street / East Street, Nassau, Bahamas, BS*). Open hours: daily Admission: free

Fort Fincastle

Fort Fincastle, which located on Bennet's Hill and can be accessed by descending the Queen's Staircase, was built in the early 1790s by Viscount Fincastle (Lord Dunmore) and offers limitless views of the town below as well as the neighboring Atlantis Resort across the lake. This historic fortification is located near the Water Tower, right off Greenwich Street, and is

surrounded by a variety of tourist stores and cafés. There are also a few huge cannons that are ideal for staged photos. The guided tours are highly recommended and last around 15 minutes. (*Address: Elizabeth Avenue, Bennet's Hill, Nassau, Bahamas, BS*). Tel: +1 242 322 7500.
Open hours: daily 08:00 to 15:00
Admission: free

Museums

After all, most visitors come to Paradise Island for the sun and sea, not for the cultural offerings. The Junkanoo Mini-Museum, which focuses only on Bahamian culture, is the only specialized museum on the island. On New Providence, in Nassau's upper reaches, there are many museums. The Pirates of Nassau, with its variety of pirate fun, and the Roselawn Museum, a little farther south, with its displays focusing on Bahamas history, are two among them.

Pirate Museum / Pirates Of Nassau

The Pirate Museum is situated on the intersection of King and George Streets in downtown Nassau, just across from the Bahamas Ministry of Tourism, and does an excellent job of recreating a true pirate settlement. The main displays include a 40-meter-long (130-foot-long) pirate ship, a pirate hall of fame, animatronic pirates, war artifacts, and treasure chests, as well as several actual objects mixed in with the glitz. This is a must-see for families with children, and you can even take a pirate tour. The nearby gift store is brimming with pirate-themed items, including a plethora of Jolly Roger flags. (*Address: Corner of King Street and George Street, Nassau, Bahamas, BS*). Tel: +1 242 356 3759. Open hours: Monday to Friday 09:00 to 18:00, Saturday 09:00 to 12:30

Admission: charge, discounts available for children

Junkanoo Mini-Museum

The Junkanoo Mini-Museum is a fantastic place to learn about the people and culture of the Bahamas, even if it isn't a must-see for the ordinary tourist. There are several spectacular exhibitions on the Junkanoo (like Mardi Gras) theme, and it encompasses Bahamian dance, music, and culture. During your stay, you may also participate in a Junkanoo jam. On weekdays at 9:30 a.m., guided tours are available. (Address: Ivern House, 31 West Street, Nassau, Bahamas, BS). Tel: +1 242 328 3786

Open hours: daily 09:00 to 17:00

Admission: charge

Public Library And Museum

The Library and Museum, which dates back to 1797, is the most historically significant government building in Nassau. This pink-hued structure, which was formerly a jail, is octagonal in design. The jail cells are now crammed with literature and significant local colonial records, as well as Bahamian treasures, shells, ancient prints, and remnants from the Arawak Indians of the past. (*Address: Shirley Street, Nassau, Bahamas, BS*)

Tel: +1 242 322 4907. Open hours: Monday to Thursday 10:00 to 20:00, Friday 10:00 to 17:00, Saturday 10:00 to 14:00

Admission: free

Roselawn Museum

The Roselawn Museum, located in the heart of Nassau, has a wealth of Bahamian culture as well as a variety of associated artifacts. This is a little attraction that covers a wide range of topics, including Junkanoo outfits. Parts of sunken Bahamian ships may also be found, as well as substantial collections of Bahamian coins, stamps, and bottles.

Open hours: daily 10:00 to 17:00. Tel: +1 242

323 318

Admission: free

Pompey Museum

The Pompey Museum, housed inside Vendue House, chronicles the life and hardships of a well-known Bahamian slave who led a failed revolt. Slave voyages to the Caribbean from Africa are also documented in the exhibits. This attraction is eye-opening for many people, especially when they witness the massive ball-and-chains that were formerly employed, the branding irons, and the animal-like collars that slaves wore, all of which date from the 16th to the mid-19th centuries. The Pompey Museum is built on the site of a historic slave sale. (*Address: Vendue House, Bay Street, Nassau, Bahamas, BS*)
Tel: +1 242 356 0495

Open hours: Monday to Wednesday, Friday and Saturday 09:30 to 16:30, Thursday 09:30 to

13:00. Admission: charge, discounts available for children and seniors

Art Galleries

While there are a few galleries amid the island resorts' various attractions, the most are nothing more than stores offering a tiny selection of art pieces. The National Art Gallery of the Bahamas, housed inside the Villa Doyle on West Hill Street in Nassau, stands out from the throng. The Chief Justice used to live in this old building, which dated back to the 1860s. The National Art Gallery of the Bahamas, which was recently rebuilt, has a large collection of paintings as well as ceramics, photos, and textiles, the most of which originate from the late twentieth century.

National Art Gallery of the Bahamas

The National Art Gallery of the Bahamas is located in Nassau, not far from Paradise Island.

This unique museum is housed in its own building and features Bahamian art, including works by award-winning modern artist Antonius Roberts and landscape paintings by Winslow Homer, a well-known American artist (1836 to 1910). Although some of the art on show may not be to everyone's taste, it is an excellent eye-opener that spans pre-colonial to contemporary times. (*Address: Villa Doyle, West Hill Street, Nassau, Bahamas, BS*). Tel: +1 242 328 5800. Open hours: Tuesday to Saturday 10:00 to 16:00 Admission: charge, discounts available for children and students

Doongalik Studios

This popular art gallery in Marina Village is a business that also serves as a gallery, and it is the only one of its kind on Paradise Island. The proprietor, Jackson Burnside, designed the Marina Village complex, and this institution is a perfect example of Bahamian culture. There are lots of contemporary art pieces for sale at the Doongalik Studios, including oil paintings by John Cox and Jessica Colebrooke, as well as other cheap modern sculptures. (*Address: Marina Village at Atlantis, Paradise Island, Bahamas, BS*)

Tel: +1 242 363 1313. Open hours: daily 10:00 to 22:00

Admission: free

Attractions Nearby

The Bahamas is essentially one large archipelago with a seemingly endless number of ways to venture out and explore the 'Out Islands.' From Nassau and Paradise Island, boat tours depart in all directions, and you may even travel to some of the larger island attractions through Nassau's airport. If you want isolation, Nassau is an excellent spot to base yourself, but please consider the various excursions and make time to visit the Great Exuma group, which has calmer beaches and much more. Eleuthera and Great Abaco are other popular destinations, while Blue Lagoon Island, which is closer to home, offers several side attractions that appeal to people of all ages.

Blue Lagoon Island

Many of the Bahamas' islands will need a plane voyage or a long boat ride to reach. Blue Lagoon Island, on the other hand, is just 30 minutes distant and is quite beautiful. Tourists are welcome to visit and appreciate the natural beauty of our private island. The island is called for the fact that it is located in a lagoon surrounded by coral cays. Snorkeling, shopping, dining, and partying are just a few of the activities available.

Great Abaco Island.

Great Abaco is one of the Bahamas' major islands, located north of Paradise Island. This island features a beautiful shoreline and plenty of scuba diving opportunities, as well as less people than Paradise Island, but Marsh Harbour, the main city, provides all of the required facilities. Treasure Cay, with its pristine beaches and sea, is another gem. Cherokee Sound, Cooper's Town, Rocky Point, Sandy Point, and Winding Bay are some of the other famous sights and places on Great Abaco, while a number of other islands (cays) such as Castaway Cay, Elbow Cay, and Moore's Island are just a short boat ride away.

Great Exuma Island.

To the south-east, Great Exuma is part of a collection of smaller islands recognized for their natural beauty. There is the occasional tourist building here, and you can fly in, but it is a world apart from Paradise Island and Nassau. The nearby Stocking Island, which lies right across from George Town and is home to the famed Salt Stone monument, as well as the Hurricane Hole, a popular cave diving destination, are also Exuma features. Stocking Island, the capital of Great Exuma, is home to a natural harbour, lovely beaches, and stunning coral reefs.

San Salvador Island / Watling Island

San Salvador is a small island off the coast of Paradise Island with windswept beaches and quiet areas, as well as historical significance. San Salvador is said to be the first island Columbus landed on in the chain, and tourists may see the cathedral (Catedral Metropolitana) and the fabled Devil's Port (Puerta del Diablo). The latter offers excellent trekking opportunities as well as breathtaking views of the island. There are also a variety of shallow-water sandy beaches and reefs for enthusiastic snorkelers.

Eleuthera.

Eleuthera Island is a long, narrow island located around 80 kilometers (50 miles) east of Paradise Island and Nassau. This peaceful island is surrounded by wonderfully blue sea and is practically unaffected by frantic tourists. Governor's Harbour and Tarpum Bay, for example, provide excellent snorkeling and there are also communities with nice amenities. The Devil's Backbone wreck is a must-see for wreck divers, while fashionistas can visit the upscale stores on Harbour Island, where famed supermodel Elle MacPherson resides.

Andros.

Andros is the largest of the Bahamian islands, nearly two hours by boat from Nassau and immediately to the west. It provides a variety of distinct topographical features. For decades, scuba divers have flocked to Andros to marvel at the 'Tongue of the Ocean' barrier reef, which is one of the world's biggest and most beautiful.

Fresh Creek is very close to New Providence, and it provides two excellent hiking routes right off the Queen's Highway, near the Small Hope Bay Lodge. With its beachside villas and sustainable-living concept, the Tiamo Resort in south Andros is a pioneer in ecotourism.

Things to Do

Medical Tourism

It was health tourism that originally placed Nassau and the Bahamas on the tourist map, and it is now a world-famous tourist destination. Medical tourism in Nassau is becoming more popular as the cost of surgery and other operations rises to exorbitant levels in Europe, North America, and the United Kingdom. The Bahamas' administration is eager to relaunch Nassau as a major participant in the medical tourism industry. With pricing for different treatments and procedures significantly cheaper in Nassau than elsewhere in the globe, combined treatment and holiday packages are gaining traction as a means to obtain high-quality medical care, and a pleasant trip may cost less than half the price of simply the therapy elsewhere.

Advantages Of Medical Tourism.

Nassau's laid-back ambiance and tropical climate are ideal for unwinding both before and after treatment, with recovery in a magnificent spa or resort setting an added plus. New and novel therapies for life-threatening conditions are effectively employed here, while they are still through the lengthy clearance procedure elsewhere. This is especially crucial for medical tourists from the United States and the United Kingdom.

Clinics and hospitals in Nassau, as everywhere, are subjected to a thorough evaluation in terms of safety, effectiveness, and ethics before being certified. Equipment, personnel, and facilities must all undergo stringent inspections. When choosing a medical tourism location, it's crucial to consider how easy it will be to communicate with medical specialists. Unlike many other South-East Asian medical tourism destinations, Nassau physicians speak and understand English.

Procedures in medicine.

Several groundbreaking treatments, including prostate cancer ultrasound therapy and a novel new minimally invasive heart valve replacement, are now accessible. Nassau has successfully conducted open heart surgery for over 10 years, and laser eye surgery is also popular. An addiction treatment center in Nassau is a recent concept. Elective orthopaedic surgery and cosmetic surgery are also offered in Nassau, with medical tourism packages sometimes combining treatment with vacations at well-known beach resorts on the islands. Certain forms of cancer may also be treated using minimally invasive laser surgery.

Hospitals.

The Doctors Hospital is the most well respected private hospital in Nassau and the Bahamas, and it just completed the Joint Commission International's four-year accreditation procedure with flying colors. It is one of just 200 hospitals in the world to get this distinguished designation. The hospital is now preparing to sell medical tourism packages in Nassau, focusing on aesthetic and elective orthopaedic surgery.

The second major hospital is the Princess Margaret Hospital, which has 400 beds and offers a variety of surgical and medical services, including cosmetic surgery and dentistry, to medical tourists.

Events and Festivals

Bahamians love to have a good time and show off their culture, so there are colorful events and festivals all year round in Nassau. The Junkanoo, a particularly Bahamian celebration, is the greatest of the lot. On New Year's Day, Boxing Day, and June, there are Junkanoos, which all include partying till the early hours of the morning. The New Year's Day Sailing Regatta, for example, is one of the sports events held on Paradise Island. The International Beer Festival (to the west of Nassau), Independence Day (in July), and the One Bahamas Music and Heritage Festival (in November) are among the other things to do and see.

January

- Junkanoo January 1st, this most cultured of Bahamian festivals takes place every year on New Year's Day, with Bahamian music, dancing and costumed parading
- New Year's Day Sailing Regatta January 1st, features a day of racing with traditional 'sloop' sailing boats at Montagu Bay (between Nassau and Paradise Island)

February

- Spring Break an ongoing pleasurable time for students during their summer break, with various sporting events, beach parties and concerts around the Bahamas
- Annual Valentine Massacre Regatta mid-February, with a day of fun activities, including sailing and partying, held each year around February 14th

March

- International Dog Show and Obedience Trials mid-March, a popular two-day event for dog-lovers both on Paradise Island and New Providence, with plenty of talented and beautiful canines on display
- Easter Celebrations late March / early April, with various religious ceremonies and processions taking place at churches around New Providence, particularly on Good Friday and Easter Monday

April

- International Beer Festival fun event at the Old Town Mall at Sandyport, with dozens of local and international beers available for sampling
- Bahamas Heritage Festival late April, cultural event with traditional music and the reciting of stories

May

- Bahamas Film Festival this ten-day event at Nassau's Galleria Cinemas showcases documentaries, videos and various movies
- Labour Day early May, a public holiday all over the Bahamas, features a variety of fun organized events on Paradise Island

June

- Junkanoo in June throughout June and July, this is a similar entity to the December / January incarnation, with much parading and Bahamian culture to be savoured by everyone in attendance

July

- Independence Day July 10th, popular day of celebration all over the Bahamas, after the country was granted independence from Great Britain on this day in 1964
- Miss Commonwealth Beauty Pageant mid-July, with a bevy of beautiful Bahamian

women vying for the title of Miss Commonwealth Bahamas

August

- Emancipation Day public holiday Bahamas-wide held on the first Monday each August, marking the day when the British abolished slavery, with lots of dressing up, and singing and dancing. Head to Fox Hill early in the morning for the fun 'Junkanoo Rush' street parade

September

- Bahamas Atlantis Superboat Challenge late September, well known international power boat race sponsored by Atlantis, featuring concerts and partying later on

October

- Discovery Day October 12th, also known as Columbus Day and National Heroes Day, when Bahamians remember the arrival of Christopher Columbus to the New World

November

- Guy Fawkes Day November 5th, the Bahamas also celebrate the burning of Guy Fawkes with masked parading during the day, and various bonfires and fireworks at night

- One Bahamas Music and Heritage Festival late November, a three-day get-together in Nassau and Paradise Island, with concerts by noted Bahamian musicians and lots of enjoyable recreational activities, including fun walks

December

- Bahamas International Film Festival (BIFF) mid-December, world-renowned film fest attracting big Hollywood names and up-and-coming local talent

- Police Band Annual Beat Retreat mid-December, with drill performances staged by the Royal Bahamas Police Force Band, held on Rawson Square and always drawing a large crowd of spectators

- Christmas Day December 25th, Christmas is celebrated with aplomb on Paradise Island, with hotels and shopping malls all getting in on the act

- Junkanoo Carnival December 26th, the third incarnation of this Bahamian cultural display, with all-night parading

Restaurants and Dining

The cuisine on Paradise Island is some of the finest in the Bahamas, but it's also some of the most costly. It's all about giant resorts and the restaurants that go with them. There is no true inexpensive eating on Paradise Island; you'll have to go across the sea to Nassau for that. The casino and the Atlantis complex itself are home to the majority of the eateries on Paradise Island. Marina Village, as well as the zone around the Paradise Shopping Plaza, are popular dining areas in addition to the shopping.

What to Eat, and where?

On Paradise Island, you may eat everything from traditional Bahamian cuisine to the best of French and Italian cuisine, as well as Asian cuisine. From reasonably affordable buffets outside of the main resorts to the best dining at the One&Only Ocean Club's Dune restaurant, which comes with a high price tag, there's something for everyone. Non-residents are welcome to eat here, but be aware that even a bottle of water can set you back considerably.

On Paradise Island, there are a few well-known French restaurants, including the legendary Café Martinique. The Bahamian Grill, which serves traditional Caribbean cuisine, offers the greatest barbecue, while the Waterfront Bar and Grill (Hurricane Hole) by the marina serves substantial meals at a reasonable price. Buffets are best found in the Market Place.

Consider dining along Bank Lane, Bay Street, Charlotte Street, Frederick Street, Hill Street, Parliament Street, and the Woodes Rogers Walk in Nassau. Head to the Gambier Village area for open-air beachside bars where you may sip a tropical beverage on a balcony while watching the spectacular ocean views.

Dining hours in Nassau and Paradise Island are not set, and they vary based on the season and the hotel's occupancy level. If you want to go posh and visit one of the expensive restaurants here, it's important to phone ahead.

Shopping

Although there are many of shopping possibilities on Paradise Island, including numerous department shops, real shopping is better done in Nassau. The duty-free shops are the most popular, and Americans often travel here for the weekend to save up to 50% on gadgets, perfume, and jewelry. Paradise Island is made up of resort malls with high-end stores and the newest styles, as well as so-called straw markets where you can get inexpensive souvenirs. The Atlantis Resort features the most stores of any resort on the island.

<u>When and where should you shop?</u>

The Marina Village, a purpose-built retail area modeled after Nassau's Bay Street, is part of Atlantis. It's great for shopping, dining, and entertainment, and it's great for a walk, however the prices on everything from apparel to jewelry, purses, sunglasses, and crafts are often exorbitant. The Crystal Court at Atlantis is located in the Royal Towers and has high-end stores like Cartier and Versace, as well as lesser-known top boutiques like Lalique, Bulgari, and Faconnable. Crystal Court is well known for its gifts and accessories. Colombian emeralds may be found in Atlantis' Beach Tower.

The Craft Centre Straw Market is another popular shopping destination on Paradise Island. Conch shells, blown glass, pottery, straw products, and colorful Junkanoo paintings are among the Bahamian handicrafts available. The Potter's Cay Market, located under the Paradise Island Bridge, is the place to go for freshly caught fish.

Other shops may be found across Nassau and Paradise Island, albeit the majority are associated with Atlantis. The Atlantis Logo

Stores, on the other hand, are suitable for more conventional products, and the Pro Shop specializes in sports gear and equipment. The majority of stores offer extended shopping hours, staying open until late at night.

Paradise Island

The beautiful, arched Paradise Island bridges connect to and from the lavish world of Paradise Island ($1 round-trip toll for vehicles and motorcycles; free for bicycles and pedestrians). The island was known as Hog Island until 1962, when it was mainly undeveloped. When Huntington Hartford, an heir to the A&P fortune, developed the island's first resort complex, he changed the name. The old high-rise hotel was renovated into the first phase of Atlantis in 1994 by South African entrepreneur Sol Kerzner. Atlantis has taken over the island after several years, a number of new hotels, a water park, and a total investment of more than $1 billion. It's easy to forget there's more to Paradise Island than the ultra-exclusive Cove and the famed golf course. Multimillion-dollar mansions and condos, as well as a few independent resort properties, may be found here. Despite the noise and bustle of the megaresorts, Cabbage Beach on the island's northern side, or the more remote Paradise Beach west of Atlantis, are also good places to enjoy peace and quiet. The island, as it has been dubbed, is a haven for beachgoers, boaters, and thrill seekers.

Amusement Park/Water Park

Long before you cross one of the Paradise Island bridges, you'll notice the striking sight of this pink fantasia. The biggest section of the Atlantis resort, Royal Towers, has a soaring sun-drenched countenance. Atlantis is as much a tourist attraction as a resort hotel, with luxury stores, a glittering casino, and apparently endless eating and drink options (40 restaurants, bars, and lounges). You can engage with dolphins, sea lions, and stingrays at Dolphin Cay. Aquaventure, a 63-acre waterpark, has exhilarating waterslides, high-intensity rapids, and a lazy-river tube ride across the grounds. At both Nobu restaurant and Aura nightclub, celebrity sightings are common. Taylor Swift, Jerry Seinfeld, and Lady Gaga have all performed at the Atlantis Live concert series, while the on-site comedy club Joker's Wild hosts prominent comedians.

Non-guests are welcome to use many of the resort's amenities, such as the restaurants and casino, but the leisure and sports facilities are reserved for resort guests and cruise passengers who purchase a ship-sponsored trip. With 11 lagoons, Atlantis features the world's biggest man-made marine ecosystem. Cruise guests may visit it on the guided Discover Atlantis tour, which starts near the main lobby at the "The Dig" museum. This fantastic collection of walk-through aquariums, themed around the lost continent and its re-created ruins, puts you up up and personal with sharks, manta rays, and a plethora of other exotic water creatures. The remainder of the trip entices you with a stroll around the several waterslides and pools that are only available to visitors. If you want to play at Atlantis while on vacation in Nassau, you must now stay at one of the Atlantis hotel complexes. Only cruise ship passengers and Atlantis-affiliated partners have access to the Discover Atlantis Tour, Aquaventure, and beach day tickets..

New Providence and Paradise Islands Restaurants

New Providence's restaurant selection is diverse, ranging from dingy shacks offering cuisine that would be found in any Bahamian's home to exquisite places where coats are worn and the food surpasses that of any big metropolis. Todd English, Jean-Georges Vongerichten, and Nobu Matsuhisa are just a few of the notable chefs with restaurants on Paradise Island.

Eating out may be costly, especially at resort restaurants, so a cost-effective method is to have breakfast at one of the many all-you-can-eat buffets at the bigger hotels on Paradise Island and Cable Beach, followed by a small snack to tide you over until evening.

Bahamian Cookin' Kitchen

Three generations of Bahamian ladies welcome visitors as though they were guests in their own house. And the Bahamian cuisine prepared in the kitchen is as near to handmade as a restaurant can get. During the week, this basic location is packed with local professionals, and it has also become a favorite "off the beaten path" destination for cruise ship tourists. Their conch fritters, according to Grandmother Mena, are the "conchiest" you'll find. (*Trinity Pl. Nassau, New Providence Island Bahamas*)

Café Martinique

Despite the fact that the original restaurant, which was made famous by the 1965 James Bond film Thunderball, has long been demolished, Atlantis has resurrected a classic with the help of renowned international chef Jean-Georges Vongerichten and New York designer Adam D. Tihany, and it is currently one of the most popular tables at the resort. On Paradise Island, Café Martinique is the pinnacle of refinement in terms of design, service, and food. The restaurant is located in the heart of Marina Village. Decor include an elevator with an iron birdcage and a wood staircase; a grand piano contributes to the elegant feel of this establishment.... The traditional French menu features basic, classic dishes that are elevated to a new level of excellence owing to the use of high-quality ingredients and the influence of chef Jean-Georges. The chef's tasting menu, which includes seven courses, is a wonderful gastronomic delight. (*Paradise Island, New Providence Island Bahamas*)

Café Matisse

At this restaurant, which is operated by a husband and wife pair who are both from the Bahamas and Northern Italy, low-slung settees, stucco arches, and copies of the same artist's works create a casually polished atmosphere. Lunch and supper may be enjoyed on the ground-floor garden beneath enormous white umbrellas, or within the century-old home if you like. To begin, start with the warm Parmesan terrine, then go on to freshly prepared pasta with crabmeat and garlic in a spicy red-curry sauce, or indulge in such delicacies as pizza frutti di mare (seafood pizza) (topped with fresh local seafood). Make sure to spare space for dessert, as well as the delectable homemade cookies that accompany with your coffee. (*Bank La. and Bay St. Nassau, New Providence Island Bahamas*)

Carmine's

If you're dining with a small party, this Italian restaurant is a terrific choice as long as everyone can agree on what they want to eat. Appetizers, entrées, and desserts are provided in extra-large servings designed to feed a big group and are served family style, making the costs more inexpensive (at least by Paradise Island standards) than they seem at first glance, particularly if you split the bill with a group of friends. The waiters can assist you in determining how many meals you should order without overindulging yourself. No matter what you pick, be sure to spare space for dessert. A chocolate cake and ice cream dish known as the "Titanic" will need everyone to work together. (*Paradise Island, New Providence Island Bahamas*)

Dino's Gourmet Conch Salad

To get a conch salad at this famous roadside eatery, get a seat, order a refreshing (though stimulating) glass of gin and coconut water, and be prepared to wait at least a half hour. If you need to go there quickly, you may phone ahead to attempt to reduce the wait time. The large number of visitors and residents who have gathered here, on the other hand, is confirmation that it was well worth the wait. Dino's is recognized with being the first to add apple, mango, and pineapple to the traditional Bahamian conch salad, resulting in the "tropical" conch salad that is now popular across the world. The view point across the street is an excellent location for taking photographs. However, here, only cash is accepted. (*Gambier, New Providence Island Bahamas*)

Grayrliff Restaurant

In this hillside mansion's formal restaurant, a dinner starts in the magnificent parlor, where beverages are served and orders made while live piano music is played throughout the room. Waiters are dressed to the nines in tuxedos, Cuban cigars and cognac are provided after dinner, and it's a privileged world. Graycliff's specialty dishes include Kobe steak, Kurobuta pork, and Nassau grouper, amongst other things. The wine cellar includes more than 200,000 bottles, many of which were hand-picked by owner Enrico Garzaroli and are worth tens of thousands of dollars each.

Despite the fact that there are many of less costly bottles, you'll discover that the markup on better vintages is far less than what you'd pay in a big-city restaurant almost anyplace in the globe. You may even purchase the world's oldest bottle of wine, a German vintage 1727, for $200,000, which is the most expensive bottle in the world. The wine luncheons held on weekdays are suitable for mere humans. You may reserve the private dining room in the wine cellar if you want to have an especially exceptional dinner experience. (*W. Hill St. at Cumberland Rd. Nassau, New Providence Island Bahamas*)

Lukka Kairi

Lukka Kairi is a Hawaiian phrase that translates as "people of the Islands," and at this trendy new restaurant, you can enjoy the delicious cuisine, live music, and warm hospitality that the Bahamians are famous for. The tapas-style menu allows you to try a range of classic Bahamian delicacies that have been given a modern touch. The crispy broccoli is an unexpected crowd pleaser, and the conch fritters are some of the finest you'll find anywhere. A must-try is the Sky Juice, which is made with chunks of toasted coconut and served until midnight at the long bar in the restaurant. If you grow weary of taking in the breathtaking view of Nassau Harbour, have a look at the mural chronicling the history of the Bahamas, which is bigger than life. Have you been having trouble understanding the Bahamian accents? You'll want to pay close attention when you enter the bathrooms because you'll learn something interesting about the island's dialect. (*Woodes Rodgers Walk Nassau, New Providence Island Bahamas*)

Seafront Sushi

This modest sushi restaurant, which is one of Nassau's most popular destinations, has an extensive menu that includes classic rolls, sushi, and sashimi, as well as more unique alternatives that integrate local delicacies such as conch. The Volcano Roll, which is topped with the restaurant's signature conch sauce, is a popular dish. Everyone in your party will be satisfied with the non-seafood alternatives available on the menu. Friday and Saturday evenings are quite crowded (and there are no reservations available), so plan on waiting for a table and for your food to arrive. (*E. Bay St. Nassau, New Providence Island Bahamas*)

Anthony's

Despite the fact that this bustling, informal establishment is one of the most reasonably priced places to have breakfast, lunch, or supper this side of Nassau Harbour, it is not inexpensive. Among the most popular items on the menu at this Bahamian and American fusion restaurant are the baby back ribs with a handmade barbecue sauce. Menu items include seafood pasta, grilled to order shrimp, grouper and salmon brochettes, steaks, burgers, ribs, and salads. There are more than 60 things to pick from on the comprehensive menu. Pizzas and a few pasta dishes are available for delivery or takeout. (*Paradise Island, New Providence Island Bahamas*)

Athena Café and Bar

Restaurant owner Peter Mousis welcomes his customers with a rousing "Opa!" He and his family provide delectable meals at reasonable rates seven days a week in their gregarious establishment. This Greek restaurant offers a welcome respite from the monotony of Nassau's gastronomic routine. Take a seat on the second level amid Grecian statues or on the balcony, which offers a great view of the scene below. A hearty Greek gyro, souvlaki, and moussaka are just a few of the dishes available at this calm and welcoming eatery. Dinner is only an option if you dine extremely early in the day; the restaurant shuts at 6 p.m. (4 on Sunday). (*Nassau, New Providence Island Bahamas*)

Blue Lagoon Seafood Restaurant

When you want a peaceful supper away from the hustle and bustle of Atlantis, this harborfront seafood restaurant is an excellent alternative. The maritime theme continues into this tiny third-floor dining area, which overlooks Nassau on one side and Atlantis on the other. Hurricane lamps and bronze railings adorn the walls, and the view from here is spectacular. Most evenings, you'll be serenaded by a one-man band, and on Thursday nights, a jazz quartet will be performing there. Choose from meals that are easily made, such as crepes filled with seafood, stuffed grouper au gratin, lobster, or stoned crab claws, to name a few possibilities. A typical Caesar salad is still available here, making it one of the few locations where you can obtain one. (*Paradise Island, New Providence Island Bahamas*)

Dune Restaurant

One & Only Ocean Club offers exquisite cuisine created by Jean-Georges Vongerichten, with a view of Cabbage Beach and views of the ocean and surrounding islands. If you want the most economical costs, go for breakfast or lunch (well, "affordable" is relative at this upscale and pricey resort). Try the Dune Breakfast, which includes eggs Benedict, french toast with mango and passion fruit, and smoked salmon, as well as other dishes. For dinner, start with a Black Plate appetizer sampler that includes everything from shrimp satay to quail to start, and finish with the White Plate sampling for dessert, which includes warm chocolate cake, passion fruit soufflé, and a variety of other delectables. Entrees such as lobster, duck, steak, and mahimahi are served with a distinctive French-Asian touch in between the main courses. It's a wonderful location to relax in the midst of the coastal breezes. (*Ocean*

Club Dr. Paradise Island, New Providence Island Bahamas)

East Villa Restaurant and Lounge

This prominent Chinese restaurant is housed in a renovated Bahamian mansion and is one of the most popular in town. A variety of entrées, such as conch with black-bean sauce, hung shew (walnut chicken), and steak kew, are available on the Chinese-Continental menu (cubed prime fillet served with baby corn, snow peas, water chestnuts, and vegetables). The New York strip steak is utopia for meat lovers. This restaurant, which is a short taxi trip from Paradise Island or downtown Nassau, is the ideal destination if you're looking for something a bit different from the normal region eateries. The dress has a casual elegance about it. (*Nassau, New Providence Island Bahamas*).

The End of Travelng to
Bahamas Guide.

Thanks for Reading.
Is my Pleasure to bring this information to
your service, and hope it serves your need.

www.ingramcontent.com/pod-product-compliance
Lightning Source LLC
Chambersburg PA
CBHW070601010526
44118CB00012B/1413